PIKES PEAK
BACKCOUNTRY

The Historical Saga
of the Peak's West Slope

by

Celinda Reynolds Kaelin

and

Leo Kimmett

ISBN 0-9651706-0-8

Library of Congress Catalog Card Number: 96-94224

All inquiries for volume purchases of this book should be addressed to:
    Twin Creek Ranch
    P.O. Box 187
    Florissant, Colorado 80816

Telephone inquiries may be made by calling:
    (719) 748-3562

CONTENTS

PIKES PEAK BACKCOUNTRY

(Map courtesy the "Ute Pass Courier")

IMPORTANT DATES IN THE HISTORY
OF PIKES PEAK'S WEST SLOPE

DATE	DESCRIPTION OF EVENT
Prehistoric to 1800s	Paleo Indians inhabit Pikes Peak area beginning 11,000 years ago. Tabeguach Utes claim the area as their hunting grounds in historic times.
1779	August 29th. Spanish Governor of New Mexico, Juan Bautista de Anza camps at Florissant while in pursuit of Comanche Chief Cuerno Verde, then proceeds down Ute Pass.
1806	November 27th. Zebulon Pike climbs either Greyback or Blue Mountain, thinking that he is ascending Pikes Peak. He cannot reach the summit.
1820	July 14th. Dr. James, a member of Major Long's topographical survey party, ascends Pikes Peak.
1846	George F. Ruxton, a young English adventurer, explores the Pikes Peak region via the Ute Pass Indian Trail.
1857	Gold is found in the Colorado Rockies, and 100,000 prospectors rush to "Pikes Peak or Bust."
1858	El Paso City (Colorado City) is founded at the base of Ute Pass.
1858	The city of Denver is founded at the mouth of Cherry Creek.
1859	Gold is discovered at "Fair Play".
1859	Ute Trail is first used as a wagon road.
1861	February 26th. Colorado becomes a Territory of the United States by Presidential Proclamation.
1862	United States Congress passes the Homestead Act.
1863	Chief Ouray and ten other Ute Chiefs negotiate the Hunt Treaty to ensure their traditional hunting grounds "forever."
1868	Gold is discovered in the Central Rockies.

IMPORTANT DATES IN THE HISTORY
OF PIKES PEAK'S WEST SLOPE

DATE	DESCRIPTION OF EVENT
1868	The Hunt Treaty is modified, and the Utes cede their hunting grounds in the Central Rockies and the San Luis Valley. Their remaining lands are ensured "forever."
1870	June 1st. Judge James Castello leaves Fairplay and establishes a Ute trading post on the banks of Twin Creek.
1871	Gold is discovered near Silverton, in the San Juan Mountains.
1871	July 31st. General Palmer plats Fountain Colony (Colorado Springs).
1872	September 2nd. Colorado Springs is incorporated as a town.
1872	December 21st. Judge Castello establishes the Florissant Post Office at Twin Creek.
1873	September 1st. Ferdinand Vandeveer Hayden begins his historic survey of Colorado.
1873	In the Brunot Treaty, the Utes cede San Juan County (San Juan Mountains) to the United States. Their remaining lands are ensured theirs "forever."
1876	Colorado becomes a state, thanks to the excitement generated by Hayden's survey.
1879	September 29th. Utes rise up against Agent Meeker on the White River, killing Meeker and nine of his men.
1881	September. The last of the Utes are forced to leave their ancestral hunting grounds in Colorado for their new reservation assigned under the Ute Agreement of 1880.
1886	July 16th. Construction begins on the Colorado Midland RR.
1886	Cascade is established as a town along the path of the Colorado Midland RR.
1890	The town of Chipita Park is established along the path of the Colorado Midland RR.

IMPORTANT DATES IN THE HISTORY
OF PIKES PEAK'S WEST SLOPE

DATE	DESCRIPTION OF EVENT
1890	Green Mountain Falls is incorporated along the path of the Colorado Midland RR. It is named for a series of cascades down the side of nearby Green Mountain.
1890	October 20th. Cowboy Bob Womack discovers gold in Cripple Creek.
1891	April 5th. Florissant's cowboys organize the Cripple Creek Mining District.
1891	January 21st. Summit Park, the stagecoach stop, is formally incorporated as Woodland Park.
1891	July 7th. Florissant becomes an incorporated town.
1891	A post office is established at George's Lake, and is named Lake George.
1892	June 9th. Hayden Placer is formally incorporated as Cripple Creek.
1894	Victor is incorporated the year following its founding by the Woods brothers, virtually on top of their Gold Coin Mine.
1895	Guffey is founded after 1894 labor strike in Cripple Creek District.
1899	Crystola is organized by a group of psychics who claim to locate gold mines by using a crystal.
1969	August 20th. Florissant Fossil Beds National Monument is established.
1991	Mueller State Park is established.

VAST FORESTS OF PONDEROSA PINE define the valleys and stream beds of Pikes Peak backcountry, while the Peak itself commands the entire eastern horizon. *(Photo courtesy Sanborn Western Camps)*

INTRODUCTION

I fell in love with the Pikes Peak backcountry the moment I saw it. I found the area totally by accident, when my husband and I took a pleasure drive west, into the mountains, while visiting my brother in Colorado Springs. At the time we were looking for a place to retire, and had almost decided to buy a ranch in my home state of New Mexico. However, Pikes Peak cast an irresistible spell upon us. One old timer echoed my sentiments exactly when he told me that he "fell in love with that Peak" when he first set eyes on her, and he had to live where "he could see her first thing every day."

I was mesmerized by her clear, frothy streams with great ponderosa pines marching along flower-strewn banks. I was enchanted by hillsides studded with magnificent granite boulders piled precariously atop one another in frozen pantomimes of turtles and Indians and frogs. And most of all, I was enthralled by Pikes Peak which commanded the entire horizon in her robe of dazzling white snow. I *had* to live in this Pikes Peak backcountry.

Certainly there are many historians better qualified to write this book than I am. And I know that there are many gifted writers who could do a better job of putting just the right words together. I doubt, however, that there is anyone who has a greater passion for the history

1

of this area, or who has found greater joy than I have in probing the mysteries of this history.

I first stumbled onto the history of Pikes Peak backcountry while in a bookstore in Reston, Virginia. Harold and I had just bought Twin Creek Ranch and were contemplating our move to Colorado. I had stopped into the bookstore for something to read during the drive, when a stack of old books on the floor caught my eye. I picked up the top book and was blowing the dust off when the book fell open. Will Drannan's account of trapping beaver in the Tarryall River Valley leaped off the page. I knew that the Tarryall River was very near our new ranch. The entire stack of books was of Colorado history, so I bought them all. Ironically, an estate in Pueblo, Colorado, had just sold them to the bookstore and now I would be taking them back to Colorado.

My daughter Jessica and her friend (also Jessica) read Drannan's book aloud during the three-day cross country drive to our new ranch. The miles flew by as we listened spellbound to Drannan's stories of trapping beaver with Kit Carson and fighting in the Indian Wars.

During the restoration of our old homestead west of Florissant, I began to research the history of our ranch. No murder mystery could have been more intriguing or exciting. So, of course, I joined the Florissant Heritage Foundation. Then, about 1993, Leo Kimmett approached me and asked if I would like to collaborate with him on a new history of the area. I had devoured every word of his book, *Florissant, Colorado,* and eagerly agreed to a joint project.

My original plan was to simply augment and revise Kimmett's original *Florissant.*

However, as each historic clue was unveiled it became very clear that the scope of the work had to include the entire area west of Pikes Peak, to the edge of South Park. Much has been written about the Cripple Creek Mining District, but many of the best stories about Pikes Peak backcountry have never been told. I eagerly embraced all of Kimmett's earlier research, and was greatly rewarded with his excellent editorial comments.

Kimmett's great-grandfather, Judge James Castello, established what is now Florissant in 1870. It was the first settlement in Pikes Peak backcountry. He fled war-torn Florissant, Missouri, in 1860 and eventually built a Ute trading post and small log hotel on the banks of Twin Creek. When he petitioned for a post office in 1872, he named it after his Missouri hometown. Judge Castello was successful mainly due to his integrity and his excellent rapport with the Ute Indians of the area. Castello gained a reputation along the Ute Pass Wagon Road as a genial and gracious host to his guests. Leo Kimmett provides living testimony to these same endearing qualities, faithfully handed down several generations. Each of our working sessions began with a sumptuous luncheon of fresh produce from his garden, loving prepared by his charming wife, Julia. This Pavlovian conditioning ensured a positive reaction from me; every time I worked on the manuscript I salivated.

Folk wisdom has long decreed that "possession is nine-tenths of the law." Politicians have pragmatically sought to implement this wisdom. Spain knew that land grants, ensuring occupancy, were vital to validating their ownership of the vast expanses that they claimed in the New World. The United States also understood this principle, and therefore passed the

Homestead Act. American Indians had no such concept of land. In their nomadic lifestyle, they harvested the fruits of the land in a cycle of successive camping grounds. Earth unfailingly nurtured her people. Earth was Mother, and it was unthinkable to own one's mother. Conflict was inevitable between the two cultures.

In order to understand a large complex issue, it is almost always easier to examine the smaller, component parts. The micro defines the macro. Fears and desires, passions and prejudices of every person combine to create the fabric of history. Each Indian, mountain man, gold seeker, and homesteader who lived in Pikes Peak's backcountry provides unparalleled insight to this westward expansion. Each of their stories tells how and why the west came to be possessed by the dominant culture, and how the Rocky Mountains were finally conquered. We are incredibly fortunate that so many descendants of these people are still living and are so willing to share their family stories and vintage photographs. We are deeply indebted to them for their generosity.

Celinda Reynolds Kaelin
Twin Creek Ranch

CHAPTER I: GEOGRAPHY AND GEOLOGY
OF PIKES PEAK BACKCOUNTRY

Nestled in a small valley at the western base of Pikes Peak, about 35 miles west of Colorado Springs and 18 miles north of Cripple Creek, lies the little mountain town of Florissant, Colorado. It is picturesquely framed by the Peak's western face. Deep green forests of Ponderosa and lodgepole pine drape themselves like a buffalo robe around the bottom of the great peak. The 14,110 foot summit of the Peak appears much broader from this western perspective. It reveals itself by a sharp, snow-capped, demarcation at timberline—looking very much like a white-cowled chieftain with head bowed and arms outstretched above its pine-treed robe.

Several streams collect the melting snows from the Peak, converging in the Florissant valley to water its grassy meadows and give life to a multitude of high mountain flowers. Chief among these streams is Twin Creek, which originates in [Hayden] Divide and then carves a dramatic path through the granite walls and boulder fields of Florissant Canyon. In the 1800s, it was known as East Twin Creek, and Witcher Creek (which joins it from north of Florissant) was known as West Twin Creek. Several other streams join the torrent of Twin Creek as it flows westward, until it finally empties its waters into the silvery threads of the South Platte

River at Lake George.

Florissant Valley rests at an elevation ranging from 8,200 to 9,000 feet, and was formed from prehistoric lake beds. This prehistoric Lake Florissant was formed when the lava and mudflows from the volcano Mt. Guffey (about 16 miles southwest of Florissant) dammed a southflowing stream around 35 million years ago. The valley area is rimmed on the south and west with other ancient volcanos in addition to Mt. Guffey. Among these volcanoes are Mt. Pisgah, Castle Mountain, Saddle Mountain, Thirtynine Mile Mountain, and Black Mountain. Eruptions from these volcanoes were probably short and violent, but they continued over thousands of years, filling the air with dense clouds of dust and fine particles of volcanic ash.

These great ash clouds were swept northwestward by the prevailing winds, and much of the ash fell into Florissant Lake, carrying ancient flying insects and foliage to the lake bottom as it settled. As one ash fall succeeded another, layers of paper-thin shale accumulated on the lake bottom, resulting in the excellent array of fossils which can be found there to this day. The perimeter of the lake was also inundated with these deep layers of ash. This silt, coupled with mud flows from the volcanoes, buried the trunks of giant trees from the immense sequoia groves that surrounded the lake 35 million years ago. Over the centuries, this mud and silt became shale, with layers up to forty-five feet thick in some places.

As the centuries passed, mineral solutions in the ground water filtered through the silt into the buried trees, silicifying and preserving them for aeons to come. According to the *New York Times*, one of the trees from this "petrified forest" measured 74 feet in circumference (at the base) and was 60 feet high when it was discovered in 1874. Experts estimated that the tree was over 500 years old when buried in ash, and that it had originally stood about 350 feet high. Early settlers reported that there were as many as sixty of these petrified trees still standing. They also reported that it was difficult to drive a wagon through the "forest" because of the numerous standing and fallen petrified trees. Experts labeled this prehistoric lake and its petrified forest "the greatest fossil field in the world." (This national treasure is now the Florissant Fossil Beds National Monument, detailed in a later chapter.)

In addition to the thousands of fossilized insects, birds and tree foliage, the fossilized remains of an ancient opossum, an oreodont (an extinct family of hoofed mammal), and a primitive horse have also been found at the Florissant Fossil Beds. In her autobiography, early resident Atlanta (Long) Thompson wrote that in the 1870s her father "was driving across the country one day when he saw some bones sticking out of a big ditch that paralleled the road. He dug them out and found them to be a rib, a tusk, and a tooth of a mastodon [This may actually have been a mammoth]. Scientists said the animal had been thirty feet high." The excitement of the 1994 25th Anniversary celebration of the Fossil Beds National Monument culminated in the discovery of the remains of a fossilized mammoth which was probably deposited during the Ice Age, and is much younger than the other Florissant fossils. Although these are the only two documented instances of large extinct animals, the Florissant area was certainly populated by many other great prehistoric beasts.

Just as the geology and geography of Florissant dictated the amassing of this fossilized wealth of 35 million years ago, it has also been the determining factor in Florissant's more recent history. For millions of years, most of present-day Colorado lay buried by the waters of a huge inland sea. These seas retreated about 65 to 70 million years ago as the Rocky Mountains appeared. The restless earth shifted profoundly, and finally thrust upward, creating the great mountain ranges of the American West. Colorado's front range, and Pikes Peak, are only a part of this upthrust. Wind, rain, and snow patiently attacked these granite monoliths, and the eroded rock debris was carried hundreds of miles and deposited along the lowlands. Glaciers along the north and east face of Pikes Peak collected billions of snowflakes over thousands of years. Then these powerful snowpacks began to sculpt the contours of Pikes Peak around 75 thousand years ago. As they crept toward the lowlands, carrying tons of boulders in a frozen, scouring embrace, they ground and carved the fault lines created by the upthrust. This combined action resulted in the steep canyons at the entrance to present-day Ute Pass. Beyond this entrance, the glaciation provided gentle u-shaped valleys leading to the summit of the pass at present-day Divide.

Soil on the western slopes of Pikes Peak is granular and red-rust in color, and is flecked with tiny specks of mica. When the winds carry these granules in their twirling dances, the sun catches the mica and gives it the appearance of swirling gold dust in the air. This unique soil is known as Pikes Peak Granite. It is the product of a large bubble of magma which boiled to the earth's surface about one billion years ago. It came to rest about 1 to 3 miles below the surface where it cooled and was gradually exposed by erosion.

As the early geographer Ellen Churchill Semple wrote "Geographic conditions influence the economic and social development of a people by the abundance, paucity, or general character of the natural resources, by the local ease or difficulty of securing the necessaries of life, and by the possibility of industry and commerce afforded by the environment." And so the story of Pikes Peak's west slope is the story of its geography.

Ute Pass (the glacially carved trail on the northern slope of Pikes Peak) provided a natural trail for the buffalo, the Indian, the mountain man, the prospector, the homesteader, the railroad and, later, the automobile. Rich volcanic activity in the region cached the great wealth of gold at Cripple Creek and the world-famous crystals and minerals found throughout the backcountry of the Peak. Shifting tectonic plates thrust up the great Rocky Mountain Range, as the elements eroded and exposed the underlying granite. Dome Rock and other grand escarpments are now ensured for the pleasure of future generations as Mueller State Park.

Florissant's prehistoric lake bed evolved into the richly flowered and gently sloping valley of Florissant, and provides a natural passageway connecting the Ute Trail to Cripple Creek in the south. The westward thrust of the valley provides a natural access to the "hunter's paradise" of South Park. This same lake bed and its treasure of fossilized remains ensured its future as the Florissant Fossil Beds National Monument. Geography has written the history of Pikes Peak's backcountry and will, no doubt, continue to dictate her future.

CHAPTER II: EVOLUTION OF A BUFFALO TRAIL

- THE UTE TRAIL

In the spring of 1839, a German doctor who "...felt the need of mental and physical recreation" decided to tour the West. He traveled from his new home near St. Louis, Missouri, up the river to Westport. There he bought a horse, a mule, and provisions for his adventure. He then joined a caravan, led by Moses (Black) Harris, which was bound for the fur trappers' rendezvous on the Green River. Dr. F.A. Wislizenus kept a diary, *A Journey to the Rocky Mountains 1839* (published in 1840). At its conclusion, he wrote an eloquent prophesy of the impact of "civilization" on the Great West.

> The ultimate destiny of these wild tribes, now hunting unrestrained through the Far West of the United States, can be foretold almost to a certainty, from the fate, already accomplished, of the eastern Indian tribes, where in the contact of races, true civilization collides with crude forces of nature, the latter must succumb. Civilization, steadily pressing forward toward the West, has driven the Indians step by step before it...
>
> So the waves of civilization will draw nearer and nearer from the East and from the West, till they cover the sandy plains, and cast their spray on the feet of the Rockies. The few fierce tribes who may have maintained themselves until that time in the mountains, may offer some resistance to the progress of the waves, but the swelling flood will rise higher and higher, till at last they are buried beneath it. The buffalo and the antelope will be buried with them: and the bloody tomahawk will be buried too. But for all that there will be no smoking of the pipe of peace; for the new

generation with the virtues of civilization will bring also its vices. It will ransack the bowels of the mountains to bring to light the most precious of all metals, which, when brought to the light, will arouse strife and envy and all ignoble passions, and the sons of civilization will be no happier than their red brethren who have perished.

Pikes Peak proved to be a vital instrument in effecting the prophecy of the good German Doctor Wislizenus. Pikes Peak is a great, granite monolith on the eastern slope of the Colorado Rockies. It presented an unfaltering beacon to Indians, Spaniards, explorers, mountain men, and early pioneers. Winding along the foot of its northern slope was the Ute Trail, a path of destiny.

A BUFFALO TRAIL

Ute Pass Trail probably had its earliest beginnings as a migratory path for the buffalo of the region, leaving their lush, grassy valleys of South Park during heavy winter snows for the milder winter pastures afforded by Colorado's eastern plains. In his *Journal of Travels Over the Rocky Mountains*, Joel Palmer wrote in 1847 that "These [buffalo] paths are remarkable in their appearance, being about 15 inches wide, and four inches deep, and worn into the soil as smoothly as they could be cut with a spade."

Dr. Wislizenus also noted the unusual habits of the buffalo.

...Where a buffalo herd has grazed for some time the ground is absolutely bare; for what they do not eat is trampled with their ungainly feet. Their bellowing can often be heard for miles. It is deeper and more muffled than that of our cattle, and at a distance not unlike the grunting of a great herd of swine. To their watering places they form narrow paths, over which they leisurely move on, one behind the other. A buffalo region is crossed by such paths in every direction.

In 1820, Major Stephen H. Long, who surveyed parts of Colorado as a topographical engineer, wrote in his journal:

> A large and much frequented road passes the springs and enters the mountains, running to the north of the high [Pikes] Peak. It is traveled principally by the bisons, sometimes also by the Indians who penetrate here to the Columbia.

AN INDIAN TRAIL

This trail was of great importance to the Ute Indians as it was one of their major "Salt Roads." This Salt Road was integral to trade because it connected the salt beds of the Bayou Salado (South Park) to the trading centers of Taos and Santa Fe.

There is a large body of evidence that the Great Shining Peak was also sacred to the Indians of the area. On Major Long's expedition in the summer of 1820, he noted the large number of Indian beads in the bubbling springs at Manitou. This was again noted by the English explorer George F. Ruxton in 1847. Ruxton wrote that "the basin of the spring [at Manitou] was filled with beads and wampum, and pieces of red cloth and knives, while the surrounding trees were hung with strips of deerskin, cloth, and moccasons [sic]."

Ute oral tradition further illustrates the numinous nature which they attributed to Pikes

Peak. According to Ute legend, the very birth of their people occurred on Pikes Peak.

In Ute language, the bear is called "quigat," and the name for the shaman or medicine man is "m'sut t'quigat"—"power of the bear." Great Spirit, God the Father, is "Sunawiv." The Bear Dance is the oldest of all the Ute ceremonies and is held each spring when the "bears wake up." Ute legend decrees that the dance was given to the people by their brother, the Bear. Bear Dance steps are an imitation of the bear as he steps forward and backward to thrust at a standing tree. Music for the dance is provided by singers who use notched sticks and a resonator to make a sound like a bear growling. The following is a poem written by Celinda Reynolds Kaelin based on a Ute legend of their nation's origins.

THE LEGEND OF PIKES PEAK

Great Spirit labored, turning large stone round and round
'Til blue sky was riven by gaping hole that he had ground.

Then down thru this funnel he poured mud, snow and trees;
Thus a great mountain grew with slopes carved by breeze.

Peak's earthen flesh sparkled with tiny stars from above
And shone a deep rust red, reflecting Sunawiv's love.

Flowers danced thru meadows and bathed their face in sun,
While Cloud People hovered to be near the bright Sacred One.

Then Great Spirit smiled, as he gazed on his tall Peak
While his beautiful daughter frolicked along a lazy creek.

She gathered fragrant blossoms in a hug to her chest,
Then lay by cool, swirling waters for a sweet, dreamy rest.

Brother Grizzly Bear saw her, in tall grass where she lay
And with plans to seduce her, he slowly lumbered her way.

A dark, handsome warrior, with long, silky hair of brown,
Made love to this comely maiden in her bower on the ground.

And when he rose from her, she cried and leapt to her feet—
In horror she saw a great, dark Grizzly in a hasty retreat.

The Ute, her dusky children, all have dark and silky hair—
To walk on all fours is how Sunawiv punished Quigat, bear.

American Indian reference to a mountain peak as "wakan," or highly spiritual, is not unique to Pikes Peak. One of the principal American Indian ceremonies is the Vision Quest, undertaken by an individual on a mountain peak for several days in seclusion and while fasting. During this Quest, it is thought that the individual will be given spiritual guidance through visions.

Colorado's Ute Indians jealously guarded their buffalo trail to South Park, building a series of small, circular forts of rough rock, without mortar, and about chest high. One of the best known of these is on Fortification Hill in Florissant.

This rock "fort" is located on a hill within the town limits, where it is supposed that the Indians fought bloody and desperate battles years ago. In the 1889 *History of the Line*, published by the Colorado Midland Railway, it was written of Fortification Hill that:

> All over the hill are breastworks built of rocks, just as the
> Indians left them, and on the side in a large rock is what has been

named The Mortise. This is a deep, smooth hole cut into solid rock. It is about 18 inches in diameter and 3 feet deep, and is suppose to have been cut by the Indians to hold water during a battle in which they might be besieged for several days.

In a story for the *Gazette Telegraph* in 1936, C.S. Dudley wrote that:

> Early settlers reported that there was a wall around the east and northern slope of the [Fortification] hill part way up from the bottom. It was a dry wall of rocks, piled one upon another. Charles Fry, a pioneer farmer of the Divide-Florissant region, who came there in 1890, says he remembers this wall; that in fact, he hauled some of the rock in it away, to be used for bridge abutments. Some of this rock also probably went into buildings in Florissant.

John Felter, in his book *The Pikes Peak People*, wrote that the Utes were reported to have built many of these rock forts along the course of the Ute Trail beginning with an area near Fountain Creek. He notes that these forts had circular walls built of rough rock, without mortar, and that they were about breast-high. These fortifications were just large enough for three to four individuals. Early residents of the area reportedly found numerous Indian arrows and other artifacts in these forts.

Irving Howbert (1846 - 1934, *Memories of a Lifetime in the Pikes Peak Region*) wrote that there was good reason for the Utes to need such fortifications.

> Every year, as far back as history or tradition goes, as soon as spring opened and grass was abundant, large parties from different tribes of the plains came marching in, and, after making their usual offerings at the "Boiling Springs," continued on

up through Ute Pass into the mountains. There the Utes usually
were waiting for them, whereupon a succession of battles between
the contending tribes would take place, with success generally on
the side of the Utes, who were the better fighters.

Kit Carson and a young man who was his foster son, Will Drannan, were to witness the

final battle between the Utes and the Comanches over the hunting rights to South Park in 1852.

(We'll discuss this battle in more detail in Chapter 3.)

In June of 1870, Judge James Castello moved from Fairplay to the junction of East and

West Twin Creeks and established a small ranch and trading post at the western base of

Fortification Hill. Judge Castello was a trusted friend of the Utes, and was well acquainted with

their famous Chief, Ouray. Mrs. Castello often had fifteen or twenty Indians at her table at one

time, and they gave her the name of "Heap Big Rocky Mountain Biscuit." Another of the Ute

Chiefs to call the Castellos "friend" was old Chief Colorow, who instructed Mrs. Castello to

send smoke signals from Fortification Hill if ever she needed his assistance. Mrs. Castello was

frequently presented with blankets, buffalo robes, and tanned deerskins by her Indian friends.

Florissant Valley was one of the favored camping grounds of the Utes until their forced

relocation onto the reservations in Utah and southern Colorado in 1880. In the winter of 1874-

1875, for example, Chief Ouray and a band of six hundred Utes camped near Florissant for

several months. Atlanta (Long) Thompson wrote that although the Utes were peaceful, their

appearance would strike terror in one's heart. Their straight, black hair always had a brightly colored hawk or eagle feather in it and their cheeks were marked with a thin vertical streak of vivid yellow and flaming red paint. Mrs. Thompson noted that the Ute camps were "very colorful because every tepee had a figure of a warrior or horse painted on one or both sides of it with the bright red, green, yellow paint that only the Indians know how to make. They usually chose a level place near a little stream where they pitched their tepees..."

TRAIL TO THE GOLD FIELDS

Ute Trail, or the Ute Pass Wagon Road, was the principal thoroughfare to the gold strikes in Central Colorado, with ample wood and water along the way. Gold strikes in Colorado's central mountains netted between 50,000 to 70,000 prospectors along the Ute Trail in 1859 alone. The Ute Trail was used primarily because the other two main roads into the gold fields were toll roads.

First among these new toll roads was the Apex and Gregory Road, constructed in the winter of 1859-60, which led to the gold fields of Black Hawk and Central City. Tolls for this road were twenty-five cents for a wagon and team, ten cents for a horse, and five cents for each head of cattle. The second of these roads was the Denver, Auraria, and South Park Road which crossed over the Platte about eight miles south of Denver, and then proceeded west into the mountains. The toll for this second road was $1.50, equivalent to the wages from a day and a half of work for the average man.

Ute Pass Trail into South Park therefore became the favored route for the prospectors headed for the gold camps. Ute Pass Trail was a very difficult road at this time, and most supplies had to be packed in on mules. Gold seekers had to leave their wagons and teams in Colorado City, at the base of the Pass, then buy mules and supplies before heading up the pass to the gold fields. As a result, Colorado City experienced a boom in its economy.

In the summer of 1860, the Colorado [City] Town Company appointed a Mr. Bott to build a new wagon road. He was asked to build the road as straight as possible, as it sometimes took as many as twenty yoke of oxen to pull a single wagon over sections of the pass. In the fall of 1860, Governor Denver of the Kansas Territory (which included Colorado) decreed that Ute Pass would also be a toll road. A cabin and toll gate were built (some report that it was staffed by the famous "Uncle Dick" Wootton) and travelers were charged one dollar per team. The citizens of Colorado City were outraged, however, and a group of vigilantes soon ran the would-be toll keepers out of town!

Colorado Springs pioneer Irving Howbert traveled the improved road with his father in 1861, and wrote that "from Denver to Hamilton our route was the same [Ute Pass Wagon Road] that father and I had gone over the year before, but in the meantime the road had been materially improved. It was not nearly so rough, and many bridges had been put in, which made travel much pleasanter."

GIANT TEN-OX, AND SOMETIMES TWENTY-OX, TEAMS such as this were often needed to pull wagons of supplies over the most difficult parts at the entrance to the Ute Pass Wagon Road. *(Photo from Underwood & Underwood circa 1860)*

In 1860, a reporter for the *Rocky Mountain Herald* wrote:

> The new free road lately completed from this city
> [Colorado City] to the Park, Blue and Snowy Range
> Diggings is the choicest, the finest, the most level,
> and the best constructed for horse, carriage or heavy
> wagon travel that there is in the country.

Ute Pass Wagon Road was so narrow, however, and traffic on it was so heavy that only westbound horses and wagons were allowed out of Colorado Springs up until noon each day, when the directions were reversed and only eastbound traffic was allowed. In 1872, a new wagon road up the Pass was completed (bypassing much of the early Ute Trail for the first thirteen miles), and it was estimated that about twelve thousand horses and mules transported freight through the pass to the gold fields each year.

In addition to its use as a freight road, the Ute Pass Wagon Road was also heavily used by stagecoaches. There were at least three coaches each week that traveled the road from Colorado Springs to Fairplay in the 1870s. Among the companies operating these stage lines were the McLaughlin's, the South Park Stage Company (Spotswood and McClelland's) and Wells Fargo and Company. Stage stops for these lines were located along the Ute Pass Wagon Road about 12 to 15 miles apart to allow for changes of horses. (These stage stations also served as polling places during elections.)

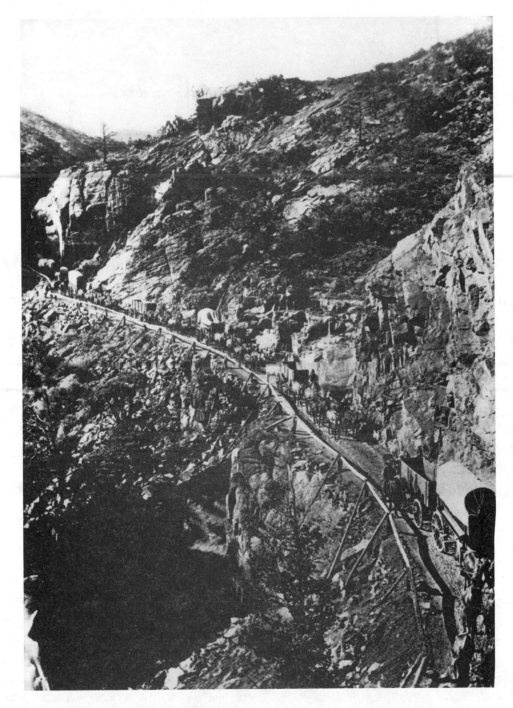

WAGONS HEADED EAST DOWN UTE PASS. Traffic was literally nose-to-tail on the narrow trail, so east

bound wagons were only allowed down the Pass in the afternoon. Mornings were restricted to west bound travelers.

(Photo courtesy Pikes Peak Library District)

THE RAILROADS

In 1870, General Palmer, who was to found Colorado Springs in 1871, organized the Denver and Rio Grande Railroad, and in 1871 began construction on that line. When the Denver and Rio Grande finally reached Leadville (by a southerly route through Pueblo and Canon City) in 1880, freighting on the Ute Pass Wagon Road declined rapidly. It was about this time that the idea of a railroad through Ute Pass was born. Colorado Midland Railroad Company (CMRR) was organized in 1883 by the owners of Aspen's Robert E. Lee Mine. Their project lay dormant until 1886, however, when John J. Hagerman (owner of Aspen's Gibson mine) became enthused with the idea and raised the money needed to build the railroad.

Construction began on the Colorado Midland in 1886, and a heated competition with the Denver and Rio Grande ensued to see which would be the first to reach the rich gold fields of Aspen. In March, 1887, construction of the Colorado Midland had already reached Florissant, but it did not arrive at Aspen until January of 1888, sixty days after the Denver and Rio Grande.

Colorado Midland Railroad was the first standard gauge railroad to penetrate the steep mountain grades of Colorado's Rockies. Hagerman bought twenty-two locomotives, thirty-five passenger cars, and one thousand freight cars for his new line. The Midland consisted of over three hundred miles of track, with some sections of 4 percent grade where it crossed the Continental Divide at 12,000 feet.

In 1891, gold was discovered in Cripple Creek, and the rush was on. Until the coming of three railroads into Cripple Creek, led by the Florence & Cripple Creek Railroad in 1894, the major transportation route for the miners and their supplies was via the Colorado Midland Railroad into Florissant, and then by stage and wagon into the new mining district.

John Hundley operated the first stage line from Florissant to Fremont (Cripple Creek), and the charge for this was $10.00 for each passenger. After Hundley started his stage line, his transportation business developed into the most remarkable stage road in the world. Eight thousand pounds of express were tugged daily over the hills and through the ravines to the gold field. Each day, fifteen six-horse Concord stages transported passengers and mail eighteen miles south to the gold strike.

In addition to the Hundley Stage Line, Alonzo Welty operated a "rickety stage" to Cripple Creek, with huge quantities of beer for the miners as his main cargo. Passengers on the eighteen-mile ride to Cripple Creek were usually afforded a break at the Welty ranch on Fourmile Creek.

In their haste to lay track for the Colorado Midland into Aspen, the engineers made an error in going over Hayden Divide, rather than going around it. This haste proved fatal to the railroad in later years. The steep 3% and 4% grades into and out of the Florissant area could have been avoided had the Midland tracks been laid in a circuitous route to the south on a more level grade. Morris Cafky, in his book *Colorado Midland Railroad,* gives a studied opinion on this error in railroad engineering.

...West of Divide, the theoretical line that should have been built probably would also have remained at a higher elevation, avoiding the steep drop into Florissant and Lake George. The maximum grade on both sides of Heyden [sic] Divide could probably have been held at 2%. But such a line was not to be. The die was cast for a steep Ute Pass location, and excessive amounts of coal and water were to be shot out of the stacks of laboring engines until the last flag was whistled in ...

Florissant would have had an entirely different history if sound construction principles had been followed in the building of the CMRR tracks. As it was, a few fateful decisions by the CMRR assured its own demise nearly forty years later. The straighter tracks of the CMRR were placed so as to find their way into the Twin Creek (Florissant) Canyon, and then directly into the south edge of the town of Florissant. The railroad brought an influx of operating personnel, their families, and a need for more housing and business—all of which radically changed the little, secluded town of Florissant. Fortunately, there are a few crisp, first-hand recollections of those booming railroad days. Morris Cafky has collected some of these colorful stories, including the following by Dr. H.A. Burton, in *Colorado Midland Railroad*.

From the time the Midland was built until it closed in August 1918, Florissant, Colorado was a busy little village which served as a helper engine station on the railroad as well as a trading center for nearby ranchers. Six helper engines were stationed at Florissant. Two of them were big 200 series 2-8-0's and the rest were 4-6-0 freight engines. The 200's were used to help eastbound trains up the 3% grade from Florissant to Divide. The smaller ten wheelers helped westward trains—two helper

25

locomotives to the train. Sometimes the 4-6-0's would help a west-bound freight to Bath, cut off and return light to Florissant. The freight would go on and pick up two more helpers at Wild Horse for the balance of the journey to Leadville. On other occasions the Wild Horse helpers would be busy helping eastbound trains up Trout Creek to Bath, or on Leadville turns. In such cases the two Florissant helpers would assist their train all the way to Leadville.

By the turn of the century, one narrow gauge and two standard gauge railroads were transporting the majority of the freight into and out of Cripple Creek. The heyday of Florissant was over, and the town gradually reverted to being simply the principle depot for the CMRR for the route between Colorado Springs and Buena Vista.

Then, in 1907, two cataclysmic events shook the economy of Florissant. Half of the town's business district burned to the ground, and a large coal mine near Glenwood Springs was abandoned, seriously depleting the now precarious freighting business of the CMRR.

The *Gazette-Telegraph* (12/17/1907) reported on the Fire At Florissant.

> Fire early last evening destroyed half the business section of Florissant, 37 miles west of Colorado Springs on the Colorado Midland railroad. Nine buildings on the west side of Castello street, the main street of the village, were burned to the ground, but the flames were stayed before they had caused further destruction. It was feared for a time that the entire town would be wiped out.
>
> The damage is estimated at nearly $20,000. Practically all of the burned buildings were the property of Daniel Nevitt, one of the pioneers of the region. Only one of the buildings was protected by insurance, this being the residence of Robert Markle, on which there was $1,000 insurance. The fire originated at 7:00 o'clock from a defective flue in Nevitt's general merchandise store and lasted for two hours. No one was injured.

Beginning in Nevitt's general merchandise store, on the corner, the fire swept the entire block. There is no organized fire department in the town, and although most of the citizens organized themselves into a bucket brigade to fight the flames, the best they could do was to prevent the fire from spreading across the street and from reaching the residence section. All of the buildings in the block were frame and the flames consumed them rapidly. None of the merchandise or contents of the buildings were saved.

The buildings burned were Nevitt Mercantile company store, containing a stock invoiced at $7,000, the Florissant hotel, a billiard hall, restaurant conducted by Mary Engle, livery barn, saloon and three dwelling houses, besides a couple of barns. These compose the entire block opposite the Midland station. On the other side of the street were the buildings of the Florissant Mercantile company, owned by F.F. Castello of this city and managed by Charles McLaughlin and James Horrigan; Allen's drug store and the post office. None of these buildings were damaged.

Mr. Nevitt, who is the heaviest sufferer from the fire, is well known in Colorado Springs and throughout El Paso and Teller counties. He is one of the earliest settlers in the Pikes Peak region, having lived here for the last 37 years. . . The fire destroyed the largest part of Mr. Nevitt's property in Florissant, although he still owns other property in the vicinity...

F.F. Castello, who is largely interested in the town, but whose interests were not harmed by the fire, last night expressed great regret upon learning the news of the disaster. "I am particularly sorry for Mr. Nevitt," he said. "He is one of the pioneers of the region, and the loss will be a hard one both for him and for the town."

In addition to the devastating fire and the closing of the coal mine at Glenwood Springs, there was more bad news for Florissant. The Denver & Rio Grande Railroad installed an improved standard gauge system into the South Park area. This eliminated the expensive process of transferring freight from their narrow gauge line onto and off other standard gauge lines, and greatly increased the Denver & Rio Grande's share of business. Previously, this had been one of the biggest advantages of shipping freight through the mountains on the CMRR. With this triple blow, the CMRR now began to experience serious financial difficulties.

On April 21, 1917, A.E. Carlton (of Cripple Creek fame) and his business associates bought the Colorado Midland Railroad at a receiver's sale for $1,425,000. Carlton began an ambitious rehabilitation program for the line in an attempt at revitalization. In the midst of this plan, the United States became embroiled in World War I. It was at this point that a governmental agency—the United States Railroad Administration—charged with controlling all railroad transportation, supplied a fatal overdose of "medication" for the ailing CMRR. Government officials had determined that the short route, from Colorado Springs to Grand Junction over the CMRR line, would provide the most efficient route for transporting troops and military supplies through Colorado.

In January of 1918 this Governmental plan was put into operation. It was doomed from the start, however, by that fatal design flaw of the too-steep grades. Colorado Midland Railroad engines were already overtaxed by the grueling mountain terrain, and could not effectively pull the added freight cars. By the middle of 1918 both ends of the CMRR line, and all side trackage between, were literally choked with stranded rolling stock. The government reacted by utilizing more reliable, though longer, railroad lines. Secretary McAdoo decreed that the railroad must cease operations, as it was uneconomical and unnecessary during the then all-out war effort. The last CMRR passenger train ran from Grand Junction to Colorado Springs on August 14, 1918. Carlton vainly tried to save at least the tracks, but a legal ruling required that they be pulled to satisfy debtors. Therefore, all of the rails were pulled in 1921. It now became necessary for the citizens of Florissant, and other towns along the abandoned line, to revert to the use of wagons and wagon roads for communication and transportation.

Once again, nature seemed to conspire with the ill fate of the CMRR as it had done in 1907, and in that same year (1921) Florissant was devastated by severe snowstorms and an ice over-flow from the normally placid Twin Creek. This ice flow destroyed most of the homes situated along the northern bank of the stream. The snows were so deep that year that Florissant was snowbound for nearly sixty days.

C.S. Dudley of the *Gazette-Telegraph* (4/18/1937) wrote of that terrible winter in 1921.

> ...South of the present Divide-Florissant road, which is the abandoned Colorado Midland grade, is the old highway [now Upper Twin Rocks Road] where Charles Fry, one of the oldest residents left in the Florissant district, one winter kept the town of Florissant in provisions when a terrific storm had it all but snowbound for sixty days, by freighting from Divide with a three-horse spike team and farm wagon over packed snow, and with banks on each side so high he could hardly see over them. At Divide lives George Pierce, the only other man who traveled that snow-banked road at that time, carrying the mail, and going on horseback when he could not get his wagon farther, often arriving at Florissant many hours overdue, exhausted and all but frozen. There used to be snowstorms that were snowstorms in the region of upper Ute Pass.

With these crippling blows from Mother Nature, coupled with the demise of the Colorado

Midland Railroad, Florissant and her sister towns once again slipped into near oblivion. In 1939 the State Highway Department built US Highway 24 along much of the old Midland railbed. Despite this improved access, however, most of the towns along the Ute Pass Wagon Road languished. Florissant even allowed its once-cherished incorporated status to lapse about this same period.

Little happened in Pikes Peak backcountry for over thirty years. Then, in 1969, the Florissant Fossil Beds National Monument was established. And in 1991 the 12,103 acre Mueller State Park was created just a few miles east of the Fossil Beds. These two attractions alone draw over 400,000 visitors up Ute Pass each year. Florissant's sister cities along the Colorado Midland Railbed were reinvigorated in 1991 when limited gaming was approved for the old mining town of Cripple Creek. Then, in 1993, Florissant was designated as the northern gateway for the Gold Belt Scenic Byways Tour.

It is the geography of Pikes Peak backcountry that has generated this rebirth. And there is little doubt that geography will dictate the future of the area, just as it has written the past.

COLORADO MIDLAND RAILROAD ENGINE NO. 14 races a Model T up the Ute Pass canyon. The train probably won this race, but the automobile eventually replaced the railroad as Highway 24 was built along the old railbed in 1939. *(Photo courtesy Pikes Peak Library District)*

Chapter II

CHAPTER III: PREHISTORIC AND INDIGENOUS
PEOPLE OF WEST PIKES PEAK

PREHISTORIC MAN

In an archaeological survey of the Florissant Fossil Beds performed in 1974, numerous prehistoric projectile points were recovered—some dating from at least 10,000 years ago. In a similar survey in 1981 of Mueller State Park a prehistoric "manufacturing" site was found. Lithic, or stone, scatter consisting of hammerstones, projectiles, and scraping tools was found, giving evidence of prehistoric (about 11,000 years old) stone tool manufacture. This is in addition to a prehistoric rock shelter found nearby, complete with its ancient fire pit and remnants of the meals cooked there.

Through these surveys, and the presence of various fossilized animal remains, we know that Prehistoric man was hunting mammoth, bison, and horse on the west slope of Pikes Peak about 5,000 years before the Egyptians even thought of building the great Pyramid at Giza.

Scientists are just beginning to understand that prehistoric man not only traveled through the high mountains of Colorado, but also lived at these altitudes. Geologist Ernst Antevs has proposed that this high-altitude living was the result of what he termed an "altithermal" period in the earth's weather patterns. During this period, the climate became much drier and warmer than at the present time, making life at high altitudes (such as Florissant) more attractive than life on the dry, dusty plains. Many noted anthropologists agree with this theory.

In October of 1993, the Colorado Springs *Gazette Telegraph* reported that the skeleton of a prehistoric man, dating from about 8,000 years ago, had been found in a cave on the White River in Northwestern Colorado. In the story, the *Telegraph* quoted Dr. Patty Jo Watson, an anthropologist, as saying that "...it's becoming apparent from this discovery and other archaeology that some of these ancient people had learned to live and work at extremely high altitudes."

Prehistoric people were hunters and gathers. They subsisted on a diet of wild game and whatever edible wild plants were indigenous to their current area of occupation. These early inhabitants depended on the herds of large animals not only for food, but also for sinew (used in sewing animal hides and fashioning weapons), and animal hides (used for clothing and shelter.) During the "altithermal hiatus," the Florissant Valley and other high mountain valleys would have provided all of the these things, in addition to another key element for survival—quartz.

Quartz was the primary resource for making projectile points, knives, scrapers, awls and other Stone Age tools. Quartz has a hardness of 7 on the mineral scale of hardness ranging from 1 to 10. Quartz is harder than the best grades of ordinary steel, which register at only about 6 on the same hardness scale. Quartz does not break apart easily, and is very tough under impact. Because of these attributes, quartz made an ideal projectile point for the deadly spears launched by early man's atlatl. This spear was fitted with a quartz projectile on one end. A short stick was then fitted with a hook made of antler or bison tooth, creating the atlatl. The flat end of the spear shaft was then fitted into this hook. A flick of the hunter's wrist and arm while holding the atlatl would then send his spear hurtling toward its target much as a sling shot hurtles a stone.

Quartz, composed of silicon and oxygen, is an igneous material, resulting from volcanic activity. Pikes Peak's western slope was a virtual cauldron of volcanic activity, resulting in numerous quartz outcroppings throughout the area. A number of prehistoric quartz quarries and workshops have been documented north of the Florissant Fossil Beds National Monument. In 1935, archaeologist Etienne B. Renaud (of the University of Denver) conducted a survey of the area and reported that the "most common type of site is the old campsite, with frequently an adjacent workshop."

Renaud also documented workshop sites within the Fossil Beds itself, "primarily on the sides of the main valley. They are frequently located on open terraces above drainages and, generally, provide a good view of the valley." Renaud reported that the lithic scatter at these sites was basically all "pure quartz, smoky quartz, quartzite, chert [a variety of crystalline silica], petrified wood, and chalcedony [milky or grayish quartz]." Since the soil in the Florissant Valley consists primarily of volcanic welded tuff material, prehistoric man must have collected this quartz from nearby quarries and then carried it to his scenic workshops to be fashioned into arrowheads, spear heads, hide scrapers, and knives.

Unfortunately, there has never been a comprehensive archaeological survey of the Florissant area as a whole. However, archaeologists have documented other, similar, high-altitude quartz quarries throughout Colorado. The most recent of these was a site near Steamboat Springs where artifacts indicated mining activity from at least 8,000 years ago (according to the September 1993 *Gazette Telegraph* story).

Near the dawning of the Christian Era, the life of prehistoric man began subtly changing as new influences filtered up from Mexico, New Mexico and Arizona. Contemporaneous with the Anasazi culture—whose beautiful architecture can be seen in the ruins of Mesa Verde, Bandelier, and Chaco Canyon—are the Fremont Indians. The Fremont culture manifested itself around 650 A.D., and then mysteriously disappeared around 1250 A.D. In *The Archaeology of Colorado*, Cassells speculates that the Fremont man probably melted into the Ute Indians. The Fremonts are thought to have occupied most of Utah and Northwestern Colorado. Scientists speculate that the 8,000 year old body of the Prehistoric man found in the White River National Forest was possibly a Fremont ancestor of Colorado's Ute Indians.

Fremont Indians practiced horticulture to some extent, although hunting and gathering were still an integral part of their life style. One fascinating aspect of the Fremont culture is their use of rock shelters. These consisted of dry-laid masonry granaries, shelters, and fortifications. The chest-high, circular rock structures of 4 to 5 foot diameter bear a striking resemblance to the remains of similar structures on Florissant's Fortification Hill.

Archaeologists have not documented the presence of Fremont people any further east of Utah than Grand Junction, but the similarities are intriguing.

THE UTE INDIANS

According to archaeologist E. Steve Cassells, the Utes were probably the earliest historic inhabitants of western Colorado, including the Florissant area.

> ... A probable reference to them by the Spanish in 1626 and a treaty in 1680 make them the earliest historically documented aboriginal group in western Colorado. An early history of New Mexico by Fray Pasados places them on the plains with the Apaches and probably in the area north of the San Juan [in the region west of Pikes Peak] and as far west as the Great Salt Lake. There is little reason to doubt subsequent accounts, including that of Dominguez and Escalante in 1775-76, which portray the Utes as the sole aboriginal inhabitants of western Colorado in historic times.

Ute legend further corroborates the prehistory of their tribe as outlined on the preceding pages, verifying the theories of anthropologists, archaeologists, and historians. This legend was recorded by T.F. Dawson and F.J.V. Skiff in the book *The Ute War*, first published in 1879.

> This legend is to the effect that the forefathers of the tribe, long years ago, lived near a vast warm lake northeast of the Big River [the Colorado]; that the country was warm, full of big trees and big deer and big oxen with white horns [mammoths?]; that big fishes and snakes as long as an hundred lodge poles abounded in

this lake; that one day all the big oxen began to roar together, and that they raised such a steam from their nostrils that the earth reeled and the sun was obscured; that suddenly the lake fell, and continued falling for three moons, and then became so much reduced that they knew it not any more, but that the big lake they found had been drained away to the south, and that its warm water had gone out through the mountains, the present canyon of the Green River and of the Big River (the Colorado); and that this old bed in the Toom-pin-to-weep, as they call the stream, is where the lake waters were drained. They also say that the story goes on that all the big deer and the big oxen with white horns strayed away eastward, and all perished in the mountains from cold or by the arrows of the Ute hunters; that soon after a big flood formed Grand River Canyon, and after this flood came a small race of people who had skin canoes, and who brought seed corn of a small kind, called in Spanish *chiquito maze*; that these people were almost white, and that they taught the Utes how to make good spears and bows and earthenware; that they built stone houses in the cliffs, and cultivated pumpkins, corn and beans; that they had silver and gold in abundance, and iron tools that they had obtained in the mountains to the northeast; that afterwards, from the northwest, came big red Indians over to this country and killed and drove off the little people, who finally all went south, as well as the big red men, who are the Apaches, Navahoes and Kiowas. They also say that the big oxen with white horns, the grande lagarios (probably alligators), were found down among the Apache and Navajo Indians, but that by and by the country became dryer and colder, and the Utes only were left on the Big River and its branches; that melted rocks were poured out everywhere and left the country desolate, and that the little people had told their forefathers that where they came from were big waters, and in these waters were men with bodies like a fish. They say that in this old river bed is plenty of gold, but that it is sure death for any one to go into the canyon to get it.

Prior to the settling of New Mexico's San Juan Pueblo by the Spanish in 1598 (nine years before the British established the Plymouth and Jamestown colonies), the Ute were a nomadic people who subsisted on roots, berries, fish and game. They lived in small family groups, spread across most of Colorado, eastern Utah, and northern New Mexico. This widely dispersed population did not mandate a cohesive political structure, and so there was none. Long before they discovered the many uses of Spanish horses, the Utes used domesticated dogs to transport their goods as they followed the migrating herds of buffalo, or to carry their goods to the different trading centers such as Taos. *The Southern Utes*, a tribal history, records the observations of an early Spaniard (1500s), Vicente de Zaldivar, who wrote of the colorful scene presented by the Utes and their dogs of burden.

> It is a sight worth seeing and very laughable to see them [the Utes] travelling, the ends of the [tepee] poles dragging on the ground, nearly all of them [the dogs] snarling in their encounter, to load them the Indian women seize their heads between their knees and thus load them or adjust the load, which is seldom required, because they travel along at a steady gait as if they had been trained by means of a rein.

Colorado's high mountain valleys and lush green plains were connected by a web of migratory trails developed by the buffalo. Certain of these trails were highly frequented by the Utes as they carried meat, hides, tallow, suet, and salt to trade with other Indians at the continental crossroads of Taos and Santa Fe. These primary trails were called "Salt Trails," and knowledge of their routes was a vital commodity. (Proper usage of salt was the only means that early people had of preserving their food over long periods of time.) These Salt Trails were noted by their unique landmarks, and their precise courses were committed to verses called "Journeysongs," a verbal type of trail map. These Journeysongs had a value of their own, and so were also traded along with other valuables of the Indian buckskin economy.

The hunting and gathering lifestyle of the Utes changed dramatically, however, with the acquisition of the horse from the early Spanish settlers. In 1637, there was an armed conflict between the Utes and the Spanish which was fought by both parties on horseback. The Spanish prevailed, and about 80 Utes were taken prisoner and held as slaves in Santa Fe. This seems to be the earliest documented use of the horse by the Utes. Later, in 1659, Ute raiding parties captured more than 300 horses from Spanish settlements in northern New Mexico. These captured horses were driven to the Ute strongholds in the Shining Mountains of Colorado. Both of these instances would seem to argue that the Ute had become expert horsemen by the first half of the 1600s. Traditional historians argue that the Ute did not acquire the horse until the 1700s. However, these two well-documented instances attest to their acquisition of the horse much earlier. In fact, it would appear from this documentation that the Ute was probably the first of the North American Indians to acquire the horse. It is even quite probable that the Utes had mastered the horse much earlier, in the late 1500s.

This hypothesis is supported by a legal agreement between the Utes and the Spanish within the terms of an interesting land control system, the *encomienda*. *Encomienda* was introduced by the first Spanish Governor of New Mexico, Don Juan De Onate, in 1598. Under this system, certain prominent Spaniards were granted authority over large sections of land. Their responsibility was to take care of the indigent Indians and to teach them Catholicism. They, in turn, were to supply men and <u>horses</u> when military protection was needed. This agreement, then, would imply that the Utes were already proficient at breeding and riding horses by 1598.

The Utes were noted as superb horsemen, and it was this love of horses that later proved so calamitous in the events of 1879. Marshall Sprague writes in *Massacre* of the Utes' horsemastership.

> No less authorities on equines than Frank Gilbert Roe and J. Frank Dobie have written that the Colorado Utes were among the first, if not the very first, North American horse Indians. Roe has stressed that most Indians who took on horses were not intrinsically altered by them. But in contrast to most, the imaginations of the Utes were fired by horses to such a pitch as to completely change their tribal personality...
>
> It was wonderful how well it worked out for the Utes. Decade by decade, the use of horses passed from Ute family to Ute family, northwesterly along their Rocky Mountain corridor, across the magnificent divides of Western Colorado and over the Uncompahgre-Tabeguache Plateau into Utah. In the process, they made a discovery; the high valleys which nobody else had wanted contained grasses of very high protein content. Using these grasses for forage, they developed a pinto pony fourteen hands high—wiry, self-supporting, sure-footed, requiring no care, and so strong as to wear out two Rio Grande horses.

There was another nutrient in these high mountain grasses that proved even more desirable than protein. It was silica. Silica is one of nature's building blocks, a mineral that vitalizes the body of horse and man by strengthening the connective tissue, skin, hair, nails and hooves. This same silica, produced by volcanic activity, is the mineral responsible for petrifying the giant sequoias in the Florissant Valley. With the ingestion of silica-rich native grasses and water, these Indian ponies became noted for their sinews and hooves of steel, and their great strength and endurance.

There were numerous conflicts between the Indians and the early Spanish settlers, and the Indians that escaped sought the safety of the mountains of Southern Colorado. In addition, the Ute began to raid the Spanish villages in New Mexico. Blooded Spanish horses were the highly valued bounty from these raids. Although the Spanish gave spirited pursuit, they were not always successful in recapturing their livestock. It was probably during these skirmishes between Indian and Spanish, and between Indian and Indian, that many of the prized Spanish horses were set free upon the mountain meadows of New Mexico and Colorado. Our modern horse is not indigenous to North America, even though the remains of prehistoric horses have been found all over the continent. Therefore, Colorado's beautiful wild mustangs are most probably the progeny of these wild blooded Spanish horses. In fact, the term mustang is derived from the Spanish word *mesteno*, which means an unbranded horse.

These mustangs thrived in the mountains and on the plains of Colorado. General Palmer, the founder of Colorado Springs, wrote of seeing three large herds of these wild horses on his trip to the Pikes Peak area in 1869. Irving Howbert, another of Colorado Springs' founding fathers (1846-1934) wrote with a pioneer's appreciation of the wild mustangs in his *Memories of a Lifetime in the Pike's Peak Region*.

> Up to the time of the founding of Colorado Springs, there were large herds of wild horses in the eastern part of El Paso County and adjacent country. Many attempts were made from time to time to capture them by use of pitfalls and other devices, but these efforts seldom were successful. One method tried with some success was to have mounted men stationed in relays at intervals of several miles over a long distance, to run down the wild horses. One of the horsemen would start the herd running at full speed in the intended direction and follow it; as the herd passed by the first relay man, the pursuer would drop out and the other, with a fresh horse, would take his place. This continued until the end of the line was reached. Then, if possible, the herd was turned back and the men who had dropped out would take up the pursuit again. This would be continued for hours with the hope of tiring the wild animals until they could be lassoed, but it never was entirely successful, for a as a rule only weaklings were captured, and they were of little value.

In his memoirs, *Black Mountain Cowboys*, author and rancher Paul L. Huntley reminisces about the mustangs of the South Park area (including Florissant) in the early 1900s. The most prized of these wild horses were those found at Black Mountain, on the south edge of South Park, near Guffey—just about thirteen miles south of Florissant. These "were good horses, some of the best winded and sure footed horses that ever walked." Huntley notes that these horses were also extremely difficult to catch due to the high altitude and the extremely rocky condition of the mountain. Most of the cowboys' saddle horses were kept on ranches about 5,000 feet above sea level. Black Mountain was about 9,000 feet above sea level, and this gave the

mustangs a great advantage, as the saddle horses became easily winded at that altitude. Huntley

recounts some of the adventure and challenge of trying to capture these wild horses.

> Most saddle horses, with a saddle and packing a man, just couldn't keep up with the wild horses. The only way was for two or more men to get after them. When you first jumped them they would run five or six miles just for the fun of it, down one ridge, then, near the end, cross over the gulch or draw then run back up. They could keep this up all day.

One of the most famous of Colorado's mustangs was a wiry little bay ridden by the

Englishwoman, Isabella L. Bird, in 1873. Bird and her horse, Birdie--"a little beauty, with legs

of iron, fast, enduring, gentle, and wise"--traveled over 700 miles alone on a sightseeing tour

of Colorado. Bird wrote fondly of her little mustang companion.

> Birdie amuses every one with her funny ways. She always follows me closely, and to-day got quite into a house and pushed the parlor door open. She walks after me with her head laid on my shoulder, licking my face and teasing me for sugar, and sometimes, when any one else takes hold of her, she rears and kicks, and the vicious *bronco* soul comes into her eyes. Her face is cunning and pretty, and she makes a funny, blarneying noise when I go up to her. The men at all the stables make a fuss with her, and call her "Pet." She gallops up and down hill, and never stumbles even on the roughest ground, or requires even a touch with a whip.

Ute assimilation of the horse into their nomadic way of life had a dramatic effect on their economy and lifestyle. Now mounted, rather than on foot, they were able to pursue bison out onto the eastern plains at the base of their Shining Mountains (the Rockies). Without the benefit of the white man's iron horse shoes, the Ute cleverly invented their own, very portable, horse shoe. They were therefore able to ride their rugged ponies throughout the Rocky Mountains with no fear of causing lameness. Ingeniously, they collected sap from the plentiful pine trees. Then they fashioned horse shoes from this sap by using a hot stone to evenly spread a gooey barrier over the horse's hoof.

Use of the horse not only increased the Utes food supply, but also provided a surplus of skins and byproducts for trade. They enjoyed an abundance of food and also a thriving "buckskin" economy. However, the structure of Ute society changed as a result. Land could now support them in higher densities. Also, their mounted lifestyle required larger numbers of people to work together in cooperation. Many family groups now began to band together.

Origins of the Ute name reflect their lifestyle prior to the advent of the horse. Ute people call themselves "Nuntz" which means "people." However, they consider the name of their tribe to be sacred, and so it is seldom if ever used in conversation. The Shoshoni called these same people "Tsiuta" which means "rabbit hunters." (John Wesley Powell wrote a detailed description of the Ute method of rabbit capture in his journal.) Early settlers and Mountain Men changed the pronunciation to "Yutas." Later usage shortened the name even more to the current "Ute."

In the late 1700s, the Ute Nation was divided into a confederation of Seven Nations: the Mouache, the Capote, and the Weeminuche, (all called Southern Utes); the Grand, the Yampa and the Uintah, (all called the Northern Utes); and, finally, the Tabeguache or Uncompahgre Utes. Tabeguache Ute claimed central Colorado, including all of Teller County, as their hunting grounds. The name "Tabeguache" is a Ute word meaning "People who live on the warm side of the mountain." "Uncompahgre" is a Ute word meaning "red water" or "red lake."

Each band, or nation, of Utes was governed by several chiefs. Usually there were war chiefs, peace chiefs, and the all-important medicine man, whose authority was comparable to a chief. Within the context of Native American spirituality, the most minute details of daily life offered a constant interaction with the Great Spirit, Sunawiv. It was understood that the Great Spirit was everywhere present, and that all things were filled with this spirit. It was further understood that all of life sprang from the earth, and therefore the land was seen as Mother Earth, and all creatures—four-legged, two-legged, winged, and water-dwelling were related as brothers. Even stones and trees and the wind were considered relations, or brothers. Ute lifeway underscored the understanding of a symbiosis of the entire universe. The medicine man was the link in communicating and understanding this symbiosis, this Oneness.

This philosophy of Oneness fomented a true democracy within the Ute social structure. When council was held, each man was given a full opportunity to discuss the question at hand. Usually, no decision was made without first reaching a consensus of opinion in council. In this way, each person's concerns and opinions were incorporated in the final plan of action.

Ute society was organized into a system of government similar to that of any contemporary American town with a mayor, city council, police force, and heads of departments. The position of head chief was analogous to the office of mayor. The head chief was generally an older and wiser man, chosen for his wisdom, courage and compassion. He usually retained his position for life. His duties were complemented by those of the war chief who functioned as the head of a police-type force. The war chief was usually a younger man who had proven his abilities in battle. In the event of any conflict, the war chief asserted his authority. However, any instigator could assemble a war party by simply informing the war chief. In other matters, however, the war chief served as the "enforcer" for the head chief. There were also numerous other subchiefs who were involved in the governing of the tribe. Central to all tribal policy, however, was the shaman, or medicine man.

Spirituality was an immanent, or intrinsic, facet of daily life. The Great Spirit controlled the roaming of the buffalo, the winds and rains, each person's health, and all subsidiary spirits—for everything possessed spirit. The medicine man therefore had the final say, after appropriate rituals, on any undertaking; for the medicine man was the communicating link with the Great Spirit.

Florissant was a favorite camping ground of one of the greatest of the Ute chiefs, Ouray. An 1886 map of Florissant shows an area designated as Ouray's campground at the western base of Fortification Hill. In the 1800s, this site would have presented an excellent campsite. It was strategically located on the northern bank of Twin Creek, with its crystal clear water and lush green meadows for the ponies. Fortification Hill lay just a few feet away, where it could facilitate the sending of smoke signals and the defense of the two trails at its base. Marksmen could be quickly placed in the rifle pits and behind the rock ramparts on top of the hill to thwart the advance of any hostiles from the North-South Oil Creek Trail, or the East-West Ute Trail. Smoke signals or mirror signals sent from Fortification Hill could be seen from Mount Pisgah (originally Signal Mountain) in the south, Signal Butte in the north, Badger Mountain in the west, or Gold Hill in the east. (There are unconfirmed reports that the Ute might have referred to the nearby Fossil Beds as the "Valley of Shadows.")

This same 1886 map also shows the open meadow east of Fortification Hill and labels it "Ute Battleground." This label was probably in reference to a fierce battle recorded in the journal of Will Drannan, the foster son of Kit Carson. Carson, Drannan and Johnnie West had been trapping in the Tarryall during the winter of 1852. Carson learned there was to be a battle between the Ute and the Comanche, and arranged to be a spectator. Carson's friend, the Comanche Chief Kiwatchee, had hoped to engage Carson and his men on behalf of the Comanche. Carson declined, however, probably because of his long friendship with the Ute. It is also highly probable that Carson's Ute friend from Taos, Ouray, was present at this battle. Ouray had left Taos to join his father and the Tabeguache Ute band in 1850. It is also very logical to assume that the battle with the Comanche was led by the Tabeguache Ute, as it was held in their hunting grounds.

This was to be a final battle between the Utes and the Comanches over the hunting right to the South Park "hunter's paradise." Drannan reports that the battle took place on the banks of a creek (probably Twin Creek) "about two miles from where it empties into" the South Platte. He also noted that this creek "heads in the Pike's [sic] Peak... and runs almost due west." Other authors have placed this battle in South Park. However, Twin Creek is the only creek in the area that meets the description set forth by Drannan—originating on Pikes Peak, flowing due west, and emptying into the South Platte. This description, coupled with the 1886 map of Florissant, would seem irrefutably to place the battle at Fortification Hill in Florissant.

Comanche warriors and their families encamped on the south side of Twin Creek, and the Utes encamped on the north side. Each morning at sunrise, the warriors of each tribe would meet along the banks of the creek and do battle, and at sunset they would carry off their dead and wounded. Through the night, neither tribe made any attempt to molest the other. But the night was "hideous with the shrieks and cries of the squaws and children of the warriors who had been killed or wounded during the day." This battle lasted four days, with hundreds of dead and wounded on each side.

Drannan assumes that the Comanche were the victors of this battle. However, there is no corroborating evidence to show that there was ever a Comanche presence in the area. It is more probable that the Ute prevailed—as usual. Historically, South Park's "hunter's paradise" and the Ute Pass Trail remained their domain until the relentless press of white miners and settlers forced them onto reservations.

Ouray, the famous Ute chief, ensured his place in history as perhaps the greatest Indian peacemaker of all time. He safely led his people through the most turbulent period of his people's history—the westward expansion of the United States. The Utes had a long history of diplomatic relations with the Europeans, beginning with the Spanish in the 1500s. Ouray capitalized on this tradition, and was instrumental in maintaining most of his peoples' lands, peacefully, from the days of the first gold strikes in 1858 until the final, climactic, Ute Agreement of 1880. While other Indian leaders in the West—Sitting Bull, Crazy Horse, and Chief Joseph—fought fierce battles and lost many lives in their bid to maintain their traditional lands, Ouray instead launched an effective diplomatic defense.

Among the Ute, however, Ouray remains a somewhat controversial figure. When the United States signed its first major treaty with the Utes in 1863—the Hunt Treaty, which wasn't fully ratified until 1868—Ouray was designated by the whites as the principal chief of the Utes. Tabeguache (or Uncompahgre) Utes, of which Ouray was the Chief, were the most numerous of all the bands at the time (numbering approximately 1500). The northern Utes were not present for the treaty negotiations, and many of the other bands did not wish to participate. Tabeguache-Uncompahgre Utes claimed most of the area in dispute, and their band represented the greatest numbers of Ute. Therefore, the United States cavalierly designated them as the "owners" and accepted Ouray's signature as legally binding for all Utes.

Chief Joseph of the Nez Perce had a similar experience with the United States government. He very eloquently explained the Indian viewpoint of such illegal tactics. Chief Joseph likened this method of "purchase" of land to the purchase of his personal horse from his neighbor, who did not participate in the ownership of the horse in any way, and who illegally sold Chief Joseph's horse after Chief Joseph had refused to sell.

Ouray, however, saw such treaties as a means to survival. In 1860, Kit Carson had urged his Ute friends to secure their lands from white encroachment by negotiating a treaty. Consequently, Chief Nevava sent Ouray to assess the impact of the white men seeking their fortunes in the Ute's Shining Mountains. Ouray traveled up the Oil Creek Trail into Florissant, then down the Ute Trail into Colorado City and Denver, and returned to Conejos through the Arkansas Valley. On this trip, Ouray found nearly a hundred thousand such gold-hungry men already in the Shining Mountains. He was convinced that it was only a matter of time before these crazed white men would take over all Ute territory. Total Ute population at this same time numbered about 4,000, and their territory encompassed all but the eastern plains of Colorado. Any reasonable person would consider these unfavorable odds. Besides, their territory was simply too large to defend against such massive encroachment. This was quite different from fighting small bands of hostile Pawnee or Comanche.

Ouray's early life provided him with a combination of skills and experiences necessary to lead his people through the traumatic transition from a free and wide-roaming nomadic people

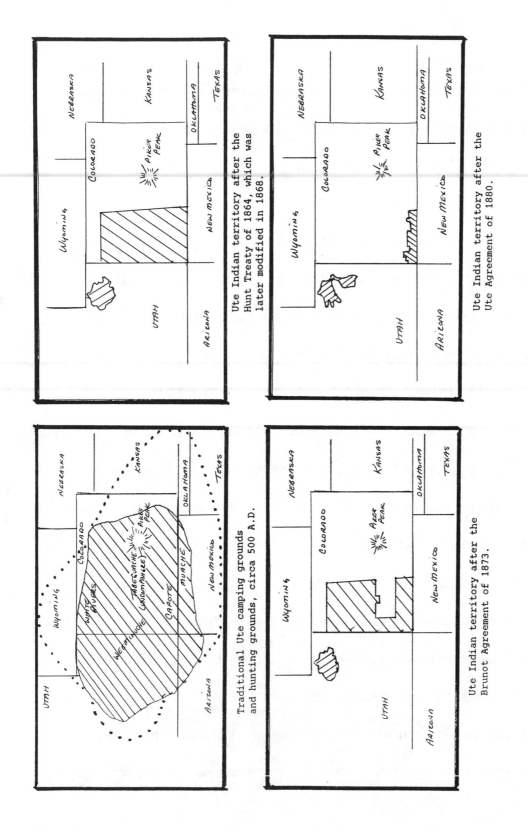

Traditional Ute camping grounds
and hunting grounds, circa 500 A.D.

Ute Indian territory after the
Hunt Treaty of 1864, which was
later modified in 1868.

Ute Indian territory after the
Brunot Agreement of 1873.

Ute Indian territory after the
Ute Agreement of 1880.

VANISHING UTE LANDS. Ancient Ute lands slipped from their control with each successive treaty they signed. Ute hunting grounds originally included virtually all of the western two-thirds of Colorado. After 1880, all Utes were confined to reservations in southern Colorado and eastern Utah. *(Illustration by CRK)*

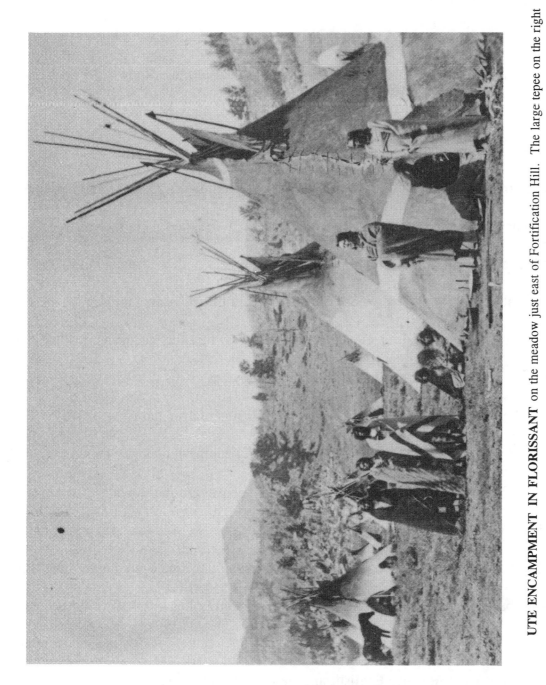

UTE ENCAMPMENT IN FLORISSANT on the meadow just east of Fortification Hill. The large tepee on the right is the Chief's, and is used for council meetings. This is probably a winter hunting camp, as everyone is huddled beneath their blanket. *(Photo courtesy Tutt Collection, Colorado College)*

to a reservation-incarcerated people.

A spectacular meteor shower, called the most brilliant such display in history, filled the night skies above the Rockies on November 13, 1833. This became known as the Year of Shooting Stars. It was also the year of Ouray's birth in Taos, New Mexico. He was the son of a Jicarilla Apache father, Guera Murah (also called Salvador), and a Tabeguache/Uncompahgre Ute mother, whose name is not known. Ouray's mother bore a second son, Quenche, a couple of year's after his birth, but she died soon thereafter. Guera Murah remarried, and he and his new wife left the two brothers with a Spanish family in Taos when Ouray was about ten or twelve years old. Guera Murah had been captured by the Utes when he was a child, and was raised as a Ute. Therefore, when the Tabeguache Ute Chief, Nevava, sent for Guera, he loyally responded, leaving his young sons behind.

Ouray and his brother, Quenche, lived with their Spanish foster family until 1850. They earned their keep by herding sheep, hauling firewood, and packing mules for the many trading caravans through Taos. At the time, Taos was a bustling, cosmopolitan town on the Santa Fe Trail. It had a colorful population of a little over 500 Spanish, Indians, French, English, American and Mexicans. Famed Indian Scout, Kit Carson, had made his home there since 1843. It was probably during this period that Carson and Ouray began what would become a life-long friendship. Ouray received a Catholic education while in Taos, and spoke fluent Spanish in addition to Ute, Apache, English, and Indian sign language.

Ouray left Taos in 1850, joining his father and Chief Nevava's band of Tabeguache. (It

54

was probably Nevava's band, including Ouray, that fought the Comanche on the banks of Twin Creek in 1852.) Sadly, it was only a short time after their reunion that Ouray's father died. However, Ouray soon became Nevava's enforcer (similar to Chief of Police) and rose to the rank of sub-chief.

Ouray was thoroughly alarmed by the number of whites he found in his fact-finding tour of 1860. Therefore, in 1862, he convinced the Tabeguache/Uncompahgre to ensure their territory against further encroachment from the whites. His negotiations with the United States government resulted in the Hunt Treaty (mentioned earlier) which guaranteed the Utes the western third of Colorado "forever," but shrinking their territory by fifty percent. With this Hunt Treaty, the Utes lost their sacred Suniwiv at Pikes Peak, along with the healing waters of Manitou Springs. Many of the Utes felt that Ouray had betrayed them. However, they continued to hunt the vast elk and deer herds of the Pikes Peak region until their final removal to the Ute Reservations in 1880 - 1881.

In 1869, Hunt was replaced as governor of the Colorado Territory by General Edward M. McCook. McCook sought to avail himself of this intra-tribal enmity against Ouray by establishing one of the lucrative Ute Agencies in Denver. Any Ute who so desired could draw his or her annuity in Denver rather than at the remote mountain Ute Agencies. Teller County's north-south Oil Creek Trail gained new importance as the anti-Ouray Utes found their way to McCook's Denver Agency.

Each month, colorful bands of Utes wound their way through the tall grass and beautiful wildflowers of the Florissant valley, past Crystal Peak, along the South Platte River and into Denver. Early Florissant maps label Wildhorn Road, north out of Florissant, as the "Ute Trail," and early Florissant pioneers speak of frequent visits by Colorow, Piah and other Denver Utes, as well as Ouray.

Unfortunately, gold was also found in the San Juan Mountains (near Silverton) in southwestern Colorado in 1871. "Forever," liberally used in prior Ute treaties, was once again amended to mean "as long as convenient." Colorado's Utes were again coerced into signing yet another treaty, the Brunot Treaty of 1873, which delineated sacred Ute lands "forever." With this treaty, the Utes ceded the coveted San Juan Mountains. Ouray wryly noted that "an agreement that a Ute makes with the United States Government is like the agreement a buffalo makes with his hunter — all he can do is lie down and die."

One can only speculate on what lands the Ute might still retain in Colorado had it not been for the actions of the rigid, over-zealous White River Indian Agent, Nathan Meeker. White River Ute Agency was located in northeastern Colorado. It boasted fertile, high mountain valleys nurtured by crystal clear streams. These lush mountain valleys provided excellent forage for Ute ponies. Unfortunately, they were also ideal for Meeker's vision of Ute farmers. Meeker developed a terminal case of tunnel vision in his quest to reform the free-spirited, nomadic Utes into farmers. Meeker blackmailed his Utes into farming by withholding their allotment food and supplies, sent by the government as payment for their lands. Tensions escalated in the conflict over converting grazing land into farm land. Finally, the situation exploded when Meeker threatened to shoot all the Ute ponies.

For the Ute, this was tantamount to genocide. The horse was not simply a means of transportation or sport. The horse was life itself. The horse ensured success in the hunt and food for hungry stomachs. The horse ensured safety from hostile tribes. The horse defined an individual's worth. The gift of horses ensured marriage to the desired woman. Foals were made a member of the household, and brought into the tepee each night to ensure their safety. The horse and life itself were inseparable.

In September 1879, the Utes rebelled, killing Meeker and ten other whites. They took Mrs. Meeker, her daughter, a farm girl and her two children captive.

Ouray rose to the occasion immediately, preventing any other Utes from joining in the uprising. His half-sister Susan was instrumental in securing the release of the captives. She boldly interrupted the council with their rescuer, General Adams, insisting that the Utes release the captives unharmed. Ironically, Susan herself had been rescued by the U.S. Army several years before the Meeker incident. She had been taken captive by the Apaches, and was about to be burned live at the stake when a Cavalry detachment gallantly raced to her rescue.

Unfortunately, the Meeker Massacre was the fatal catalyst in Colorado's smoldering cauldron of anti-Ute sentiment. General Philip Sheridan's pronouncement that "the only good Indians I ever saw were dead" was echoed in virtually all of Colorado's newspapers. Senator

Henry Teller declared that Ute genocide was the only possible solution. The citizens of Greeley

(of which Meeker had been a founding father) passed an anti-Ute resolution.

> Resolved, As the sense of this people, that the Indians within the
> limits of our State are a hindrance to its proper development, and
> a constant menace to the safety of the people; that by their recent
> unprovoked and inexcusable depredations they have forfeited all
> claims to remain among us; and we insist as our ultimatum in this
> matter that the death penalty be inflicted upon the fiendish
> murderers of our friends; and that the Utes be speedily removed
> beyond the borders of Colorado.
> Two hundred thousand people pray for this result.

Colorado's public, led by Senator Teller and the press, were demanding Ute genocide.

Bowing to public pressure, the United States Congress passed the Ute Agreement of 1880. This

"Agreement" provided for the removal of all Utes from Colorado to reservations in Utah and

southern Colorado. However, Ouray's efforts to secure the release of the hostages and to

prevent further bloodshed were somewhat rewarded in the Ute Agreement of 1880.

> The Uncompahgre [Tabeguache] Utes agree to remove to
> and settle upon agricultural lands on Grand River [Colorado
> River], near the mouth of Gunnison River, in Colorado, if a
> sufficient quanity [sic] of agricultural land shall be found there; if
> not, then upon such other unoccupied agricultural lands as may be
> found in that vicinity and in the Territory of Utah.

This area was not only extremely fertile agricultural land, but also carried special

spiritual significance for the Ute. Grand Mesa was known to the Ute people as "Thigunawat,"

the home of departed Ute spirits, and was very sacred land.

Otto Mears, the infamous entrepreneur of Colorado's toll roads and high-altitude railroads, had himself appointed to President Grant's commission which enforced the treaty. Earlier treaties provided that subsequent treaties could only be ratified by a three-fourths vote of all Utes. In 1881, Mears was charged with bribery for paying two dollars in cash to every Ute that signed the treaty. However illegal, Mears did succeed in obtaining the required number of votes. Mear's treachery did not stop here. He led the commission in requiring that the Tabeguache Utes be co-located with the White River Utes on the Uintah Reservation in Utah.

Treaty provisions for a special Tabeguache reservation at the junction of the Colorado and Gunnison Rivers was completely ignored. In fact, later that same year the area was declared public land. This extremely fertile farmland then became the location of the city of Grand Junction which was incorporated in 1882. Fortunately, Chief Ouray died before this last betrayal by Mears. His efforts to bring peace and prevent further bloodshed after the Meeker uprising were ultimately repaid with lies and theft.

Sadly and ignobly, the nomadic lifestyle of the Ute was tragically and abruptly ended. It is a bitter irony that the Ute hunting grounds on the western slope of Pikes Peak, where they valiantly fought the Comanche on the banks of Twin Creek, were later named Teller County after the strident anti-Ute politician, Senator Henry M. Teller. In a further irony, the Colorado Midland Railroad wound its way through Ute Pass and along the Ute Pass Trail adorned with the image of a noble Ute warrior as the railroad's logo.

CHIEF OURAY AND HIS WIFE, CHIPETA. Ouray skillfully used diplomacy and treaties to retain the ancient lands of his people longer than any other Indian nation. After Ouray's death, Chipeta joined Chief Colorow's band, renounced the white man's ways and again lived in the traditional Ute way. *(Photo courtesy Denver Public Library)*

COLORADO'S SENATOR HENRY M. TELLER. Teller County's namesake. Teller and Jerome B. Chaffee were the first U.S. senators from Colorado. *(Illustration from 1888 "Harpers Weekly")*

CHAPTER IV: EARLY EUROPEANS AND AMERICANS

ARRIVE IN THE FLORISSANT AREA

SPANISH ADVENTURERS

On August 29, 1779, the Spanish governor of New Mexico, Juan Bautista de Anza, camped in the Florissant valley while in pursuit of a marauding band of Comanches. De Anza had set out from Santa Fe on the 15th of August with 600 men. Five days later he was joined by about 200 Utes and Apaches who begged for the chance to combine forces against the Comanche. (It was the Ute who named the Comanche. Comanche, or Komantcia, is a Ute word meaning "Anyone who wants to fight me all the time.")

29 August 1779 Sunday At eight o'clock, the weather still bad, we forged ahead to the east [from Johnson Village at Buena Vista]. In this direction and through a good country four leagues [about twelve miles] were made. These over we paused in a good arroyo, as much to refresh the riding beasts as to give time to all people of the expedition to prepare and dress the meat of fifty head of buffalo they had succeeded in killing in less than ten minutes from the great number which broke in on our march [in South Park].

...After these scouts had been sent out at the time spoken of, we again took up our route at six in the afternoon to the east-southeast. Along it six leagues [eighteen miles] were made through good country, with many small streams. The day's journey terminated, the night now being well advanced, at the foot of a hill which was called Los Ojos Ciegos [in Florissant].

Los Ojos Ciegos, or Blind Eyes, probably refers to Twin Rocks, a prominent landmark along the Ute Trail in Florissant. Two house-size, oblong boulders appear as though suspended in the pine trees, visible for miles before reaching Florissant. The rocks were probably named Los Ojos Ciegos in reference to the Ute legend of a very proud coyote who thought to impress others with the trick of making his eyes leave his head on command. However, he did the trick once too often, and his eyes were left hanging in the pine trees, never to return to their sockets.

Angry Comanches had been raiding Spanish settlements in northern New Mexico during the latter half of the 1700s in an attempt to drive the Europeans back to Mexico. The fateful provocation in 1779 was led by a brash young chief, named Cuerno Verde. "Cuerno Verde" in Spanish and Ute means Greenhorn. In a skirmish at Ojo Caliente (north of Santa Fe) in 1768, the first Comanche Chief, Cuerno Verde, was killed by the Spanish. His son vowed to avenge his father's death, and so assumed his father's name and his distinctive headdress. The name was reflected by the headdress, which was made of leather and green-tinted buffalo horn.

The two adversaries—De Anza and the younger Cuerno Verde—were perhaps destined to meet. In a fate somewhat similar to that of Cuerno Verde, both De Anza's father and grandfather had been killed while fighting the Apaches in Sonora, Mexico. His resolve was a match for the notorious Comanche's aggression. De Anza noted that Cuerno Verde's own "nation accuse him, ever since he took command, of forcing them to take up arms and volunteer against the Spaniards." Cuerno Verde's own men called him by the Comanche name Tabivo Naritgant, or "Dangerous Man."

Florissant was an ideal resting spot along De Anza's campaign route. The valley was large enough to accommodate the camp needed for over 800 men in addition to providing plenty of grass and fresh water for their 2400 horses and mules. De Anza continued his pursuit down Ute Pass, or Sierra Almagre [Red-Ocher Mountains], through what is now Colorado Springs and then south along Fountain Creek, or Santa Rosa—so named by the Spanish. (The Spanish also called upper Fountain Creek, which cascades from Pikes Peak above Manitou Springs, the Rio Almagre.) After a successful skirmish just north of Pueblo, De Anza finally encountered Cuerno Verde a few miles south of Pueblo, and defeated him on the banks of Greenhorn Creek—named after this famous Comanche chief who died on its banks. Greenhorn Mountain, just east of Interstate 25 south of Pueblo also bears the name of this Comanche Chief. With the defeat of Cuerno Verde, De Anza was able to secure an enduring peace with the Comanche.

At the time of the fateful altercation between De Anza and Cuerno Verde, the Spanish presence had been felt in the New World for over 200 years. It wasn't until 1565 that Spain established its first settlement in what is now the United States, almost 73 years after Columbus first encountered the Americas. This colony was established at St. Augustine, Florida. However, the first Spaniards in the American west were refugees from a failed colony in Florida, who inadvertently landed in Texas near Galveston Island in 1528. They had fled Florida, and had hoped to find safe sanctuary in Mexico, but a storm blew them off course. These Spaniards, led by Cabeza de Vaca, spent six years wandering through Texas and Northern Mexico before being reunited with their compatriots in Mexico.

In 1538, the Viceroy of New Spain, Antonio de Mendoza, sent a Franciscan monk, Marcos de Niza, to explore the region north of Mexico. De Niza returned from his quest within a year, telling incredible stories of a city of great wealth, "bigger than the city of Mexico." Incited by the fabulous wealth of the Incas in Mexico, the Spanish were all too ready to believe and to exploit. By 1598, Don Juan de Onate led over 500 men, women, and children up from Mexico to establish the first Spanish colony in the west at San Juan Pueblo, just north of Santa Fe. The Spanish Pope, Alexander VI, had given all of the "New World" to the Spanish Crown in 1493, and so the Spaniards of New Spain felt it their right and imperative to ensure ownership through colonization as quickly as practicable.

Meanwhile, in 1682, the French explorer, Robert Cavalier, sieur de La Salle, set out from Canada to explore the Great Lakes and the Mississippi River. During this foray, La Salle laid claim to the entire Mississippi drainage for his king, Louis XIV of France. This drainage included the Platte and Arkansas rivers, which carried the waters from the eastern slopes of the Rockies down into the Mississippi.

When the English established their colonies at Jamestown in 1607 and at Plymouth Rock in 1620, they claimed sea-to-sea boundaries, from the Atlantic Ocean to the Pacific Ocean.

Colorado lay in the center of this territory disputed by Spain, France and England. Spain was generally accorded ownership of all of Southern Colorado, up to the Arkansas River, and all of western Colorado, again with the Arkansas headwaters defining the boundary. Pikes Peak's west slope, and all of eastern Colorado belonged to the French. At the end of the French and Indian War in 1763, the Treaty of Paris awarded all of Colorado to Spain. So for a brief period, Pikes Peak's west slope became Spanish territory. Then in 1800, Napoleon forced Spain to return the Louisiana Territory (including central and eastern Colorado) to France, and so the Peak's west slope was once again French territory.

However, in 1803 Napoleon sold the Louisiana Territory to the United States for $15 million, and so the slopes of west Pikes Peak finally found permanent ownership with the new Republic.

West Pikes Peak country still bears many traces of its multi-national past. Along with the colorful pioneer names such as Cripple Creek and Tarryall, there are traces of the Spanish influence in such names as Colorado (meaning "red") and El Paso (originally "El Paseo," meaning the pass) County. Teller County was part of El Paso County until 1899, when the new county was created. El Paso was the original name of Colorado City at the base of Ute Pass, for Ute Pass was originally known as "El Paseo". Pikes Peak was named "El Capitan" by the Spanish, and was used as a prominent landmark demarcating Spanish territory. French trappers named the headwaters of Fountain Creek in Manitou Springs the "Fontaine que Bouille" (meaning the Stream That Boils). South Park was first known by its French name, Bayou Salado (Salt Marshes). The Platte River was so named by the French because of its very "flat" appearance.

Colorado Springs pioneer Irving Howbert writes in his *Memories of a Lifetime in the Pikes Peak Region*:

In corroboration of the claim that Spanish expeditions passed over the town site of Colorado Springs at a very early date, is the following incident. While digging a cellar at 529 East Pike's Peak Avenue in June, 1894, workmen uncovered, some six feet below the surface, an iron box four by six inches in size, which was rusted to the point of disintegration. This iron box held a crucifix, attached to which was a Maltese cross having a small erect cross as a pendant. The two crosses were made of dark colored stone resembling chalcedony, while the crucifix was of solid brass hammered. All these articles were hand made showing the hammer marks and filed edges. None of the three bore any inscription or date, but evidently had been lost by some priest accompanying one of the early Spanish exploring expeditions.

Van E. Rouse, secretary of the Board of Education in Colorado Springs at the time of the discovery, happened to be watching the excavation when the iron box containing the crosses was uncovered, and obtained possession of them. It was Mr. Rouse's purpose to give them to the El Paso County Pioneer Association for its historical collection, but before this was done they had mysteriously disappeared. However, they had been seen by many people, myself included. The loss was most unfortunate, for these old Spanish crosses were relics of great historical value.

ZEBULON MONTGOMERY PIKE

El Capitan, the great peak, was later to be re-named for the man whose writings made it famous, Zebulon M. Pike, rather than for the American who first climbed it, Dr. Edwin James. The swirling mists of political intrigue have obscured the historical truth of Zebulon Montgomery Pike in much the same manner that the swirling winds of snow and cloud obscure the great mountain peak that bears his name.

In July of 1806, Pike was sent to explore southwestern Louisiana Territory by General James Wilkinson. Pike set out with about seventy-five men, mostly Osage Indians. Their starting point was near St. Louis, Missouri, where Pike followed the Arkansas River west into Colorado. In November, he was offered his first glimpse of the 14,110 mountain that would come to bear his name. Pike wrote that "At two o'clock in the afternoon I thought I could distinguish a mountain to our right which appeared like a small blue cloud." Actually, he had to travel another 150 miles over a period of twelve days before his party actually encountered

ZEBULON MONTGOMERY PIKE, NAMESAKE OF PIKES PEAK. In 1806, Pike attempted to climb the "grand Peak," but had to abort the attempt as his men "were in every way ill provided to endure the inclemency of the region." *(Illustration courtesy Pikes Peak Library District)*

the mountain. When they finally drew near enough, Pike and three other members of his party set out to climb the peak. On the fourth day of the attempted assault, they were forced to abandon their efforts.

>*27th November, Thursday*. Arose hungry, dry and extremely sore from the inequality of the rocks on which we had lain all night, but were amply compensated for toil by the sublimity of the prospects below. The unbounded prairie was overhung with clouds which appeared like the ocean in a storm, wave piled on wave and foaming, whilst the sky was perfectly clear where we were. Commenced our march up the mountain and in about an hour arrived at the summit of this chain. Here we found the snow middle deep, no sign of beast or bird inhabiting this region. The thermometer which stood at 9 [degrees] above 0 at the foot of the mountain here fell to 4 [degrees] below 0. The summit of the Grand Peak, which was entirely bare of vegetation and covered with snow, now appeared at the distance of 15 or 16 miles from us, and as high again as what we had ascended, and would have taken a whole day's march to have arrived at its base, when I believe no human being could have ascended to its pinical [sic]. This with the condition of my soldiers who had only light overalls on, and no stockings, and every way ill provided to endure the inclemency of the region; the bad prospect of killing anything to subsist on, with the further detention of two or three days, which it must occasion, determined us to return.

After Pike aborted his attempt to climb Pikes Peak, he led his expedition further west along the Arkansas, then up the west branch of Oil Creek Trail, through what is now Elevenmile Reservoir, and into South Park. They then turned south and crossed into the San Luis Valley. This caused great consternation among the Spanish, who captured Pike and his men and held them prisoner for over a year before they were repatriated.

During Pike's absence, General Wilkinson was revealed to be deeply enmeshed in the treasonous plot with Aaron Burr to create their own empire in the western Louisiana Territory. Burr was tried for treason in 1807, but was acquitted. Pike was tainted by his association with Wilkinson, but was finally cleared of any unpatriotic deeds by the War Department in 1808. In 1810, Pike published a highly popular record of his adventure, titled *An Account of Expeditions to the Sources of the Mississippi, and Through the Western Parts of Louisiana, to the Sources of the Arkansaw, Kan, La Platte, and Pierre Juan Rivers*. His account was also sold in England, France, and Germany—whetting the European appetite for the romance of the western frontier.

MAJOR STEPHEN H. LONG

The War of 1812 not only ended Pike's life, but also created a hiatus in exploration of this western frontier. It wasn't until 1820 that the Secretary of War John C. Calhoun sent Major Stephen H. Long to explore the Rockies. After exploring along the front range, the party arrived at the Great Peak. The party's botanist, Dr. Edwin S. James, together with a soldier and a wagon master, decided to climb the peak. They finally succeeded late in the afternoon of July 14th, 1820. When they returned to their base camp, Major Long decided to confer the name of "James Peak." The name did not stick, however. This was probably due to the popularity of the writings of Pike that had been previously published and widely circulated.

JAMES PURCELL

Actually, Pike had been preceded in Colorado by another American, James Purcell of Kentucky, whom Pike referred to as "Pursley." Pike met Purcell in New Mexico, and recorded his story for posterity. Purcell had set out from St. Louis with a few companions in 1802. They spent three years trapping and trading with the Indians, but not without incident. Pike wrote of one such very colorful happening. Some Indians had stolen Purcell's horses, and he and his friends followed the thieves into their village. Pike relates that "The horses were there, but the Indians refused to give them up. Pursley saw his horse, with an Indian on him going to the water at the edge of the town, pursued him, and with his knife ripped open the horse's bowels. The Indian returned to the village, got his gun and came and snapped it at Pursley, who pursued him into the village with his knife. The Indian took refuge in a lodge surrounded by women and children. This struck the chiefs with astonishment and admiration for the 'mad Americans,' as they termed them, and they returned the other horses to the hunters."

Later, while Purcell was in the midst of trading with the Comanches and Kiowa on the Eastern plains of Colorado, they were attacked by a band of Sioux. They fled into the mountains, probably by way of Ute Pass, through Florissant. Purcell remained in South Park, where sometime around 1805, he claimed to have discovered gold. He is said to have later discarded the yellow metal when it became too cumbersome, as it was of no value in the remote areas of his travels. When Pike encountered him in Santa Fe in 1807, Purcell was working as a carpenter. He apparently was immune to the metallic fever which ruined so many lives during the second half of the 1800s.

GEORGE FREDERICK RUXTON

One of the most remarkable American travelers through the Florissant area was a young Englishman, George Frederick Ruxton. Born near Oxfordshire, England, Ruxton's spirit of adventure was thwarted and stifled by the conservative atmosphere of English society and countryside. He wrote in *Adventures in Mexico and the Rocky Mountains* that "I was a vagabond in all my propensities. Everything quiet or commonplace I detested and my spirit chafed within me to see the world and participate in scenes of novelty and danger."

When just seventeen, Ruxton fought in the Spanish Civil War, winning the Cross of the Order of San Fernando. He then returned to England and enlisted in Her Majesty's Eighty-ninth Regiment. When shipped for duty in Canada, he became bored with barracks life and sold his lieutenant's commission. He then reveled in the life of a hunter in the deep forests of upper Canada. After a brief visit to England, he set off on two separate trips to Africa. Ruxton could not resist the romance of the Mexican War, and so in 1846 set sail for Veracruz. From there he journeyed up to Santa Fe, and thus began his two-year adventure in the mountains of Colorado. He traveled extensively, up Ute Pass, into Florissant and throughout the Pikes Peak area, writing of this primitive freedom.

Although liable to an accusation of barbarism, I must confess that the very happiest moments of my life have been spent in the wilderness of the Far West; and I never recall, but with pleasure, the remembrance of my solitary camp in the Bayou Salade [South Park], with no friend near me more faithful than my rifle, and no companions more sociable than my good horse and mules, or the attendant cayute which nightly serenaded us. With a plentiful supply of dry pine-logs on the fire, and its cheerful blaze streaming far up into the sky, illuminating the valley far and near, and exhibiting the animals, with well-filled bellies, standing contentedly at rest over their picket-fires, I would sit cross-legged enjoying the genial warmth, and pipe in mouth, watch the blue smoke as it curled upwards, building castles in its vapoury wreaths, and, in the fantastic shapes it assumed, peopling the solitude with figures of those far away. Scarcely, however, did I ever wish to change such hours of freedom for all the luxuries of civilised life; and, unnatural and extraordinary as it may appear, yet such is the fascination of the life of the mountain hunter ...

Young Ruxton died in St. Louis in 1848 of epidemic dysentery at the very young age of twenty-seven. Fortunately, Ruxton provided vivid accounts of adventures of the Mountain Man in both *Life in the Far West* and his autobiographical *Adventures in Mexico and the Rocky Mountains*. Ruxton was the first author to write extensively of the Mountain Man. His colorful and authentic portrayals of fictional La Bonte and Killbuck created a new romance of these heroes in fringed buckskin.

MOUNTAIN MEN

Dr. LeRoy Hafen, former Director of the State Historical Society of Colorado, wrote that "Trappers and traders were the trail makers and path finders of Colorado, the real pioneers of the rocky Mountain West... It was the trapper's persistent search for beaver and the trader's urge to barter with red men, that unlocked the geographical secrets of the western wilds and eased the way for official explorers and for settlers."

There were a few impediments, however, which precluded the rich beaver pelts of South Park and the Florissant area from the fortunes of would-be trappers. The Louisiana Purchase of 1803 loosely defined the new American borders as laying north of the Arkansas River. The area south of the River was still claimed by Spain, which actively discouraged incursions by "foreigners" into its territory. Santa Fe and Taos—centers of Spanish commerce—were also the closest trade centers for any would-be trappers to exchange their beaver pelts for cash. This exchange, however, required a grant, or license, from the Spanish government. These grants were sparingly awarded, and were usually given only to Spanish citizens. Without access to the markets in Santa Fe and Taos, trappers were forced to travel east, the full distance of the Arkansas River, to the bustling markets in St. Louis.

Beaver hats were the height of style, however, in both the Eastern United States and in Europe, and fashionable, monied society was prepared to pay handsomely to indulge its tastes. At one time a single beaver pelt brought as much as thirty dollars; thirty dollars represented an entire month's salary for the common man of this period. The extreme profitability of this luxuriantly furred, web-footed rodent spawned the golden age of the Mountain Man, from the early 1800s until the mid 1800s.

The demise of this golden age was foreshadowed with an act of the United States

Congress, the "Trade and Intercourse Act" of 1834. This act was intended to preserve the resources and way of life of the American Indian from further encroachment by the white man. Among these protected resources was the beaver. During the golden age of trapping, however, most conflict between the whites and the Indians was averted mainly through the proclivity of the beaver to grow its thickest fur, and therefore most valuable pelt, during the harsh Rocky Mountain winters. The American Indian, dependent upon the migrating buffalo and other seasonal sources for food, generally abandoned the deep winter snows to follow these food sources to the somewhat warmer valleys and plains at the base of the mountains.

In the way of all things since the beginning of commerce, it was economics which finally ended the romantic era of the Mountain Man. Silk top hats became the fashion and beaver pelts, which had sold for as much as thirty dollars each, fell in value to less than three dollars each in the late 1830s. The American Fur Company, organized by John Jacob Astor in 1808, ended its mountain business with a final Mountain Man rendezvous in 1839 on Horse Creek in Wyoming. The last of all the Mountain Man rendezvous was a small, dispirited affair held on Wyoming's Green River in 1840.

CHOUTEAU AND DEMUN

In the late 1700s and early 1800s, St. Louis, Missouri was a small village. Because of its strategic location, it was the fur trade center for the western frontier. It is not surprising, then, that August Pierre (A.P.) Chouteau, the grandson of one of its founding families, would be among the first to harvest the rich and abundant beaver pelts of Pikes Peak's backcountry.

A. P. Chouteau was outfitted by his younger brother, Pierre Junior (Cadet), in 1815 for a fur trading expedition into the Rocky Mountains. Cadet's company, Berthold & Chouteau, was later (in 1827) to become the sole western agent for Astor's powerful American Fur Company. A.P. Chouteau and his brother-in-law, Jules DeMun, traveled into the Rocky Mountains to the sources of the Platte and Arkansas Rivers (Teller County and South Park areas) to trade with the Comanches, Arapahos and Utes. The trip was a financial disaster that presaged further problems between the brothers. These culminated in an 1838 lawsuit wherein Cadet won a settlement against August Pierre for everything that he owned.

Cadet's business ventures into the fur business of the Rocky Mountains carried the dissonance of the brother's unhappy relationship. When Cadet sent his partner's son, Sylvestre Pratte, to Taos in 1826 to take charge of 120 free trappers, he again met with severe financial losses. These trappers ranged as far north as the Platte River and Lake Utah, exploring every tributary and stream of the Upper Arkansas drainage, which included the Florissant area. Though these trappers spent two years gathering their furs, they had little success, and the venture was viewed as a calamity by Cadet.

CAPTAIN JOHN GANTT

Indians of the Rocky Mountain area were first introduced to the insidious poison of alcohol by a dishonored ex-Army officer, Captain John Gantt. Gantt was dismissed by the Army in 1829 for falsifying pay accounts, and sought his fortune in trapping the headwaters of the Arkansas in the South Park area. During the winter of 1832, he and his party of trappers built a log stockade on the Arkansas River near the mouth of the Purgatory (about 70 miles east of Pueblo). He established a trade with the Indians of the area, persuading them to drink his sweetened whiskey. In 1834, he moved his operations six miles east of Fountain Creek (present-day Pueblo) on the Arkansas River, and named it Fort Cass. His trade with the Indians was challenged by Bent, St. Vrain & Company who built a fort three miles further east on the Arkansas. Gantt was no match for their competition, and abandoned his fort and trading business about 1835. Bent & St. Vrain also abandoned this location, and rebuilt their fort another seventy miles east on the Arkansas River to its current location just outside of La Junta. (This fort is also a recent reconstruction, as the original was destroyed by an explosion and fire in 1848.)

One of the more famous trappers working with Gantt during this period was none other than Kit Carson. Carson and Gantt trapped the South Park area, working in the Florissant Valley and then east down Ute Pass, during the winter of 1833.

KIT CARSON

Christopher "Kit" Carson began life inauspiciously as the third son--and sixth of eight children--born to a Revolutionary War veteran and his Kentucky bride in 1809. His father was killed when Carson was but nine, and four years later his mother remarried. There was friction between the new stepfather and young Kit, and so he was apprenticed to a saddle maker in Franklin, Missouri. In 1826, at the age of seventeen, Carson ran away, joining a wagon train bound for Santa Fe. Thus began the legend of the man who was to become a Mountain Man, Indian Agent, and renowned explorer--the Christopher Columbus of the West.

In 1829 Carson received his first taste of the freedom and romance of the Mountain Man when he joined Ewing Young's trapping expedition to Arizona and California as camp cook. Carson was an apt pupil, however, and was Young's trusted lieutenant by the time they arrived back in Taos two years later. He then set out with the famous trapper, Thomas Fitzpatrick, in 1832, and made what was probably his first incursion into the Florissant area. Later that year, he left Fitzpatrick and joined Captain John Gantt--who Carson refers to as "Captain Gaunt" in his autobiography. Carson and Gantt trapped the South Park and Florissant area throughout the next year, 1833. Carson then spent the next ten years trapping in the company of some of the West's most famous Mountain Men--including Jim Bridger and Old Bill Williams.

It was also during this period that Carson had his first taste of battle with the American Indian. Mountain Men were the interlopers, traveling and trapping illegally in the mountains of the West, which the United States government had designated as belonging to the American Indian. Indians dealt harshly with these hairy-faced, buckskin-clad intruders, usually setting them afoot by stealing all of their horses and at other times, taking their lives. Carson soon learned that by striking back swiftly and firmly, he and his men were usually able to prevail— even when the odds were ten or more against one. However, Carson's later fame as a proficient and eager Indian Fighter is strangely at odds with his other dealings among his unwilling American Indian hosts.

While it is true that he fought a great many battles against hostile Indians, it is also true that he was married to two different Indian women at different times. His first wife was a beautiful Arapaho girl named Waa-nibe, or "Singing Grass." She bore him a daughter, Adaline, about 1837 and then a second daughter sometime later. This second daughter died at three years of age when she fell into a kettle of boiling soap in Taos. Waa-nibe was spared the agony of seeing this helpless child die, for she herself had died shortly after giving birth. Carson then married a beautiful Cheyenne girl known as "Making Out Road" sometime around 1841. He had fought a deadly duel for her hand with another of her suitors, an overbearing French bully named Shunar. Carson killed his rival, and won the hand of the Indian princess. However, this marriage seems to have lasted only a few months, and ended with a bitter fight. In January of 1842, Carson was baptized a Catholic and then in February of 1843 married Marie Josefa Jaramillo of Taos. His brother-in-law was the ill-fated Governor of New Mexico, Charles Bent. It is interesting that Carson does not mention either of his Indian wives in his autobiography. However, genteel society at this time would have been outraged by anyone married to what they considered to be a "savage."

One of Carson's many foster children, Will Drannan, gives us another glimpse of Carson's relationship with the American Indian. In their travels together, Drannan wrote that they were most always met by the Chief of the nearest village, and were required by frontier etiquette to attend a very specially prepared Dog Feast and then to smoke the peace pipe.

Typical of their reception at the different villages was Drannan's description of an encounter

with a band of Comanches as recounted in his memoirs *Thirty One years on the Plains and in*

the Mountains.

> We were met on the outskirts of the village by White Horse, Chief of the Comanches, who, being an intimate friend of Uncle Kit, shook hands with us and conducted us to his own wick-i-up. There we unpacked the animals and piled up our goods, and White Horse detailed an Indian to guard the packs day and night.
> After our horses had been picketed out to grass, the Chief took us into his lodge to dine with him, and here again we had boiled dog and the peace smoke.

Carson and Ouray, the famous Chief of the Tabeguache Utes, were good friends through

some of the most critical periods in Ute history. They probably knew each other from their

early days at Taos—Ouray having lived there from the time that he was ten years old (1843) until

he was about seventeen (1850). Carson had married Marie Josefa Jaramillo at Taos in 1843,

and they made their home there until they moved to nearby Rayado. In December of 1853,

Carson was named the Ute Indian Agent at Taos and served in this capacity until his resignation

in 1861 in order to enlist in the Union Army. Ouray replaced Nevava as Chief of the

Tabeguache Utes in 1860, having first served as Subchief for an extended period. As Subchief

and Chief he would have worked closely with Carson.

CAPTAIN WILLIAM F. DRANNAN (foster son of Kit Carson) as an adult poses with his favorite horse, Black Bess. *(Photo from Drannan's "Thirty One Years On the Plains and In the Mountains)*

Through this friendship, Carson urged his friend Ouray to seek a treaty with the United States Government to ensure well-defined boundaries to sovereign Ute Territory. The timing of this treaty was critical, as gold had been discovered near Denver in 1858; near Leadville and in the Tarryall Valley in 1859; and near Durango in 1860. Colorado's mountains were swarming with tens of thousands of whites suffering from "gold fever." Adding to this pressure,

KIT CARSON, PROBABLY THE WEST'S MOST FAMOUS SCOUT. This artist's rendering shows a very young and handsome Carson, clearly in his prime. *(Illustration from 1862 "Harper's Weekly")*

Colorado became a Territory in 1861 and then Congress passed the Homestead Act in 1862. These two actions sent additional thousands of whites into the Rockies with "land fever."

Ouray and his friend, Kit Carson, began work almost immediately on a Treaty to protect Ute lands. The Ute were successful in negotiating this treaty with the Governor of the Colorado Territory, and in 1863 what would later be known as the "Hunt Treaty" was signed. The United States Congress did not ratify this Treaty, however, and in 1868 Ouray and nine other Ute Chiefs traveled to Washington for further bargaining. Ouray persuaded his good friend, Carson, to accompany them although Carson was seriously ill at the time. A number of changes were made to the Treaty, mostly to the disadvantage of the Utes.

This Treaty came about mainly through the friendship of Carson and Ouray. (This Treaty was discussed in greater depth in Chapter 3). Through it, the Utes maintained their life-giving hunting grounds in Florissant and the South Park area, even though gold and land fever raged through the Rockies coupled with strident cries of "The Utes must go!"

The Civil War also created a complex and unfortunate climate for the Indians of the West. The Confederate government strove for strategic advantage by embroiling the Choctaws, Chickasaws, Creeks, Seminoles and Cherokees as allies in their battle with the North. In Minnesota, angry Sioux took up arms against the whites when the promised annuities of their treaties were interrupted by the Civil War. In New Mexico, militant Navajo seized the opportunity of a distracted Union Military to launch fierce attacks on New Mexico settlements.

Brigadier General James H. Carleton, commander of the Department of New Mexico, was keenly aware of the vulnerability of the white settlers under his protection. With an economy of men and materials dictated by the profound battle waging between the North and the South, Carleton devised a simple and effective "scorched earth" policy in dealing with the Indians. Under Carleton's direction, Colonel Kit Carson led the First New Mexico Volunteer Cavalry, conquering both the Mescalero Apaches and the Navajo. In a final, fateful march against the Navajo in 1864 through Canyon de Chelly, Carson effected a devastating scorched earth campaign. Carson then oversaw the controversial and deadly Long Walk, relocating the now starving Navajo to the Bosque Redondo in eastern New Mexico. With this final blow, the Navajo Wars ended.

Carson received a final command at Fort Garland (Colorado) in 1866, and was mustered out of the Army in 1867. He joined his family at their farm near Las Animas (at Boggsville) for a much needed rest. A horse had fallen on him in a hunting accident in 1860, and he had never fully recovered from the injury to his chest. His friendship with Ouray mandated the trip with him to Washington, D.C. in 1868 in order to assist in the treaty negotiations. Carson returned to his ranch, exhausted, and suffering with an aneurysm in his chest. Two days after his return, Josefa gave birth, then tragically died ten days later. Kit followed his beloved wife exactly one month later, on May 23, 1868.

There were a number of Mountain Men whose exploits equaled or exceeded those of Kit Carson. However, Fate chose to cast Carson in a different light. It was Carson's service to the Pathfinder of the West, John Charles Fremont, that catapulted him into the public's eye and international fame. Carson met Fremont on a Missouri river boat in 1842, and offered his services as guide through the Rockies. Fremont had been selected to head this expedition by his father-in-law, Missouri Senator Thomas Hart Benton. Benton had plotted for years to expand the western borders of the United States, and felt that Fremont's reconnaissance of the area would make it more attractive to Americans. Carson led Fremont over the South Pass (along what was later known as the Oregon Trail) in 1842 and again in 1843. In 1845, he joined Fremont for a third trip to California, this time remaining with Fremont to fight against the Mexicans until his return in 1848. It was Fremont's *Report*, published in 1845, that captured the imagination of the American public and launched Carson into the pages of history.

Carson's biographer, Harvey Carter, wrote in *Mountain Men and Fur Traders of the Far West* that "...there is less difference between the real Carson and his legend than is usually the case with frontier heroes. This is because Carson was really a man of many admirable qualities and few reprehensible traits and because he really did lead a strenuous and adventuresome life."

WILLIAM F. DRANNAN

It is generally agreed among Carson's biographers that he took under his protection as many as twenty homeless young boys. These "foster" children were of all races—Anglo, Spanish and Indian. This was probably his way of healing himself of the pain he had experienced when his own widowed mother remarried and he ran away from his unhappy home.

Perhaps the most famous of these foster children was William F. Drannan. Drannan was born on the Atlantic Ocean to French emigrees on their way to America in 1832. They later died in the cholera epidemic of 1836, leaving four-year-old Will and his seven-month-old sister. The orphaned Will was taken in by a plantation owner by the name of Drake whose lands bordered on those of General Andrew Jackson near Nashville, Tennessee. Young Drannan was quartered with the Negro slaves, and was greatly mistreated. He never was able to learn what became of his baby sister.

In Drannan's autobiography *Thirty One Years on the Plains and in the Mountains*, he asserts that he ran away from Drake in 1847, finding his way on foot to St. Louis where he met Kit Carson. It is because of the controversy over this date that many historians disparage the veracity of Drannan's memoirs. They argue that Carson was in California with Fremont in 1847, and so Drannan's account must be manufactured. If, however, one views Drannan's account as having erred in the date by five years—making it 1842—then the remaining events in Drannan's life do appear to be logically truthful.

It was in 1842 that Carson took his young Indian daughter to a boarding school in St. Louis, and had his fateful first meeting with Fremont. This also seems more logical in light of Drannan's actions. He writes that he met Carson in the lobby of a hotel where he had gone to inquire for a job. Carson took note of him when he began to cry after his request for a job was denied. In the 1800s, a fifteen year old was usually considered a man, and to cry as a child would be unthinkable—no matter what the provocation. Tears from a fifteen-year old would have hardly engendered the sympathy of Kit Carson nor induced him to take such a soft young man as a fledgling Mountain Man. This is, however, the more probable response from a ten year old, which Drannan would have been in 1842.

Drannan's memoirs were first published in 1900, over fifty years after his experiences with Carson. They were written without benefit of a journal, and were composed almost entirely from memory. Even Carson's autobiography errs in many of the dates that he assigns to events. This is a natural, but not necessarily fatal, flaw in writing from memory. Drannan's book was quite popular. It sold very well, and this sheer volume of sales subjected Drannan to broad public scrutiny and validation. His book survived this rigorous test, and was even republished several times.

Drannan's memoirs provide an interesting insight to the true character of Kit Carson, and also paint a vivid picture of their years trapping in Pikes Peak backcountry.

In October of 1842 (Drannan lists as 1847), Carson, Drannan, and Johnny Hughes traveled up the headwaters of the Arkansas, where they built a winter cabin on a "stream that empties into the Arkansas." (This could have been near Currant Creek or Four Mile Creek in southern Teller County. The timing of this trip would have allowed for Carson's first trip with Fremont from June to August of 1842.)

Drannan writes that Carson's method of establishing a trapper's camp for the winter was to enter the area on horseback with plenty of packhorses for the provisions. These horses were then sent back with a hired man once the destination was reached. On subsequent trips, this remuda was simply pastured nearby during the winter months. The use of pack animals allowed for a number of comforts in the winter quarters. Drannan reports that the "cabin" was sometimes made entirely of logs, and at other times was a log cabin partly bermed into the earth, and was generally about twelve feet square. Its roof was made of small pine logs, covered with brush and pine boughs, then covered again with dirt. A crude door was fashioned out of hewn logs, fastened together with crossed pieces held together with wooden pins. This whole affair was then hung on heavy wooden hinges.

A small portable wood stove was used for cooking and heating, and a crude bed was made out of a green elk hide which was fastened to a rough-hewn log frame. By immediately sleeping on the green hide, it shaped itself to one's body providing "first class comfort."

Each trapper had responsibility for a dozen traps, or a string. These traps were carried around in a "trap sack" made of stout buffalo skin. Early Mountain Man Joe Meek left a detailed account of the business of trapping beaver in his memoirs *No Man Like Joe*.

> ...[the trapper] has an ordinary steel trap weighing five pounds, attached to a chain five feet long, with a swivel and ring at the end, which plays round what is called the *float,* a dry stick of wood about six feet long. The trapper wades out into the stream, which is shallow, and cuts with his knife a bed for the trap, five or six inches under water. He then takes the float out the whole length of the chain in the direction of the center of the stream, and drives it into the mud so fast that the beaver cannot draw it out: at the same time tying the other end by a thong to the bank. A small stick or twig, dipped in musk or castor [an oil taken from the beaver's glands] serves for bait, and is placed so as to hang directly above the trap, which is now set. The trapper then throws water plentifully over the adjacent bank to conceal any footprints or scent by which the beaver would be alarmed, and going to some distance wades out of the stream.
>
> In setting a trap several things are to be observed with care: first, that the trap is firmly fixed, and the proper distance from the bank—for if the beaver can get on shore with the trap he will cut off his foot to escape; secondly, that the float is of dry wood, for should it not be the little animal will cut it off at a stroke and swimming with the trap to the middle of the dam be drowned by its weight. In the latter case, when the hunter visits his traps in the morning, he is under the necessity of plunging into the water and swimming out to dive for the missing trap and his game.

These traps were monitored each day (some were as far as seven or eight miles from

MOUNTAIN MAN SETTING HIS BEAVER TRAPS. Trapping beaver was a frigid business, as the best pelts were obtained in the winter months. Success required that the "trapper wades out into the stream, which is shallow, and cuts with his knife a bed for the trap." *(Illustration from 1862 "Harper's Weekly")*

camp) when the drowned beaver were removed, skinned, and the traps were reset. The skins were then stretched by making a bow of a small willow or other pliant sapling, and then pulling the hide over this frame. As the hides dried, they were removed from these frames, and then packed in another frame for transport, with fifty "plews" to each bale.

Only the barest of necessities were packed in for the winter's camp--coffee, sugar and flour became only fond memories after the first few months. Trappers fed themselves with whatever game could be found within the area. Beaver tail was considered quite tasty, and if nothing else, provided diversity in an otherwise bland diet of other fresh meat. The cold mountain streams of the Rockies freeze solidly for only brief periods during the winter, usually no more than six weeks. Trappers used this forced hiatus to make enough moccasins, gloves, shirts and leggings from their elk hides for the remainder of the season. (Each trapper required at least twelve pair of moccasins each year.)

Trappers always left their camp in early spring as the snows began to leave the mountain valleys. This early departure usually insured ample separation between the return of indigenous Indians of the area and the departure of their unwelcome winter guests.

Drannan trapped for Carson for almost ten years, making numerous forays into the Rockies for the bounteous beaver skins. Their final trip together was to South Park and the Tarryall in 1852. They traveled over Ute Pass and struck South Park on the east side, probably at Wilkerson Pass. Drannan wrote glowingly of his first view of South Park.

> ...a more beautiful sight I never saw than the region was at that time. Coming in from the direction mentioned, one could overlook the entire park, which was almost surrounded by snow-capped mountains, and the valley, several miles below, which was about eighty miles long and from ten to twenty miles wide, was as green as a wheatfield in June. When we were near the valley we could see elk in bands of a hundred or more, with small herds of bison scattered here and there in the valley, and antelope by the

hundreds.

I had often heard of a hunter's paradise, and when I got sight of this lovely valley, with its thousands of wild animals of almost every description known to the continent, I made up my mind that if there ever was such a place as a hunter's paradise, I had surely found it. The high mountains with scattering pine trees on the sides; the snowy white peaks above the timber line, and the many little mountain streams and rills that paid tribute to the main stream that coursed this beautiful valley, all combined to form a scene of magnificent grandeur. The quaking-asp, balm and various other kinds of small timber that grew along the streams all helped to add to the beauty of the scene.

This last winter's camp was made in the Tarryall river valley, just north of present day Lake George. Drannan writes that this was the winter when a large herd of bison in the valley nearly trampled him to death when they stampeded. The following spring was also eventful in that he and Carson witnessed the final, decisive battle between the Ute and the Comanche in Florissant. (Drannan's vivid account of this battle was recounted in Chapter 3.)

Carson and his friend Lucien B. Maxwell "rigged up a party of eighteen men to go trapping" on this expedition as a final farewell to their lives as Mountain Men. Besides Carson, Maxwell, Drannan, and Johnnie West, it is not known who the other members of this party were. They split into groups of three and four, and established cabins about four to eight miles apart. (A trapper's cabin dating from this period is still standing at the Twin Creek Ranch in Florissant. Another trapper's cabin, bearing Carson's carved signature and dating from this period, is located on Black Mountain near Guffey.)

Drannan writes that "Aside from my race with the bison, I put in a very pleasant winter [1852], and Uncle Kit said he had never spent as pleasant a time in the mountains as he did that winter in South Park. 'In fact,' said he, 'it was more like a pleasure trip than anything else.'"

CHAPTER V: JUDGE CASTELLO BUILDS

A TRADING POST

From 1852 until 1859 there was a brief respite from the white man's intrusions into Pikes Peak's backcountry. Beaver were no longer threatened by hairy-faced trappers, and so they rebuilt their dams in the gently coursing waters of Twin Creek. Great blue heron stalked the sandy stream bed, searching for food as noisy flocks of Canada Geese built their nests in the willows along the banks.

Coyotes slunk through knee-deep grama and wheat grass, pouncing on the large snowshoe hares who fed there. Golden eagles, bald eagles and peregrine falcons gently glided on thermals from the valley, preying on unwary prairie dogs and ground squirrels. Thousands of mountain blue birds searched for tiny bugs among the grasses as the sun magnified the hue of their lazurite wings.

Small herds of buffalo marched along the Ute Trail as billowing clouds of black and brown Buffalo Birds followed in their wake, leaving their orphaned eggs in the nests of the songbirds along the trail. A myriad of brightly colored butterflies and hummingbirds flitted among meadows choked with delicate blue wild iris and columbine.

Deer, elk and antelope calved and nourished their young on the silica-rich grasses growing among the fallen petrified trees. Bear wandered through the timbered hills surrounding the valley, feasting on a bounty of wild blackberries, cow currants, and rose hips. Mountain lions stretched lazily atop the huge boulders in Twin Creek Canyon, luxuriating in the warm mountain sun.

Mustang ponies whinnied to one another, periodically interrupting the peace of this idyllic mountain retreat as they carried dusky hunting parties into the valley. Grassy banks along Twin Creek turned host to a multitude of buffalo-skin tepees, gently glowing like Mexican *luminaria* under the stars, as the cooking fires were kindled and succulent fresh game was roasted.

Then, in late 1857, a Delaware Indian, Fall Leaf, presented a quill of Colorado gold dust to a merchant in Lawrence, Kansas and the fate of the Rocky Mountains was sealed. During the next two years, gold seekers came swarming over the Shining Mountains. Soon the gentle tendrils of blue smoke from 6,000 Ute tepees were totally obliterated by the black smoke from 100,000 prospector's campfires. This was the state of the mountains in 1860 when Chief Ouray made his fact-finding journey which resulted in the Hunt Treaty.

Twenty-year old Charles Castello was among those with visions of gold dust in their eyes. He traveled from Florissant, Missouri to the Gregory Diggings at Central City by ox team in 1859. He must have been impressed by what he saw, for he was joined the next year by his forty-six-year-old father, James Castello. James also must have been favorably impressed, as he soon sent Charles back to Missouri for the sole purpose of returning with the remainder of the Castello family. James worked the Nevada Gulch near Central City, then moved on to the diggings near Fairplay. He was joined there in 1863 by his wife, Catherine Hughes Castello, and their five other children—Lucy Ann, James, John, Andrew, and Francis (Frank). Charles, however, chose to remain in Missouri.

It is very likely that Catherine Castello was relieved to have her husband and oldest son out of Missouri during the Civil War. Missouri, far from the bloody battlefields of Virginia, was nonetheless a hotbed of Rebel guerrilla warfare. Catherine Castello told her grandchildren many stories of ambush killings, of crying Negroes who did not want to be freed, and of Missourians' deep-seated hatred of Lincoln.

Catherine Castello exemplifies the early pioneer woman in her faith, courage, and sturdy ability. Fearless and trusting, she left her comfortable home in Florissant, Missouri, at her husband's summons. Despite the rigors of winter, she gathered her five children and her household goods and boarded the train for Atchison, Kansas. James sent two trusted guides, John and Aaron Ripley, to meet Catherine at the train and accompany her by ox cart to Fairplay —a dangerous journey of sixty days through the mountains. As the wagons approached the line demarcating the Colorado Territory, Catherine lined up her children, gave each a good scrubbing, and dressed them in their best. She dressed five-year old Frank, the youngest, in a new pair of red velvet pants, which she had made for this special occasion.

The Castellos soon settled into the vibrant life of the Fairplay gold camp. By 1866, there were about 200 residents and a thriving brewery. James and Catherine established the Castello Hotel—a charming two-story log building which also hosted the town's meetings.

JUDGE JAMES CASTELLO, circa 1865. Judge Castello was a genial man and a gracious host to travelers who stopped at his trading post on the banks of Twin Creek. In 1872, he established a Post Office there and named it Florissant after his hometown in Missouri. *(Photo courtesy Myrtle Dalby)*

CATHERINE HUGHES CASTELLO, (MRS. CASTELLO), circa 1865. Mrs. Castello was famous for her hearty home cooking, especially her biscuits. She made her log cabin hotel as comfortable as possible, lining its wall with canvas and illustrated newspapers. *(Photo courtesy Myrtle Dalby)*

James, who had been sheriff in St. Louis, was soon acting as County Judge. In 1865, Judge Castello became a member of the first State Senate of the Colorado Territory. In 1868, he was appointed by President Johnson as receiver at the newly established United States Land Office in Fairplay. As receiver, Judge Castello acted as "banker" for the US government, collecting and depositing all federal monies. He served in this capacity until 1872.

Social life for the Castellos soon revolved around their two eligible daughters, who were quickly married off. In 1865 Lucy Ann married George W. Barrett, a freighter who later became one of the few prosperous miners at Hamilton on the Tarryall River. Then Mary Castello married William H. Beery in 1866. Beery was a teamster along the Ute Pass Wagon Road. He and Mary later established the Thirty-Nine-Mile Ranch along Currant Creek, just about thirty miles south of Fairplay.

It was also during this time at Fairplay that Judge Castello became involved as an agent for the Colorado Superintendency of Indian Affairs. When Congress passed the Homestead Act in 1862, thousands of land-hungry settlers pressed in on the Indian lands. (This was in addition to the thousands already scouring the mountains for gold.) Government officials made hasty new treaties every few months in order to placate the Indians. In these treaties, the Indians were guaranteed annual supplies and monthly rations "forever" in exchange for their lands. An Indian Bureau had been established under the War Department in 1790 to control these commercial relations, but this control was later transferred to Congress in 1834. The annual budget of the Indian Bureau soared to over five million dollars. Suddenly, the fragile business of Indian relations became Big Business, and an excellent venue for buying votes.

This new Indian Bureau required a virtual army of contractors, agents, freighters, warehouse owners and distribution clerks. With so many jobs, and so much money at stake, the Indian Bureau became a key pawn in the game of political patronage, and abuses were rampant. President Johnson sought to lend an air of nobility and integrity to Indian relations in 1869 by placing the nomination of Indian Agents in the hands of church societies. Unfortunately, most of these "godly" men proved to be as corrupt as their secular counterparts. Judge Castello, however, proved to be the exception to this rule. He became a trusted friend of the Utes and their leaders in a friendship that would grow and deepen over the years.

In 1861 an Agency for the Tabeguache Utes was established at Conejos with Lafayette Head as Agent. Head had been run out of his native Illinois by his neighbors when he married a twelve-year-old girl. He escaped with her to Colorado, where she later died. He then married a wealthy, vivacious Spanish widow and settled near Conejos in 1854. He became an early cattle baron and a very powerful man. The Utes, however, accused Head of stealing supplies intended for them and then substituting the shipment with spoiled provisions. Cattle that were designated for the Utes were euphemistically called "slow elk" and shot by hungry miners. Otto Mears (who later replaced Head as Agent at Conejos) derisively called these cattle bearing the Ute USID brand (United States Interior Department) the "USID—U Steal, I Divide" beef.

Agent Head shrewdly hired Chief Ouray as his interpreter for the princely sum of $500 a year, hoping that this would enhance his relationship with the Utes. The winter of 1864 had been brutal for the Tabeguach Ute people, as heavy snows prevented them from gathering their winter supply of buffalo meat. As a result, they were reduced to begging for food. In November, Utes and settlers had been shocked and outraged by Colonel Chivington's ruthless attack on Black Kettle's peaceful Cheyenne encampment at Sand Creek, east of Colorado Springs. Over one hundred and fifty Indian men, women and children were killed. Chivington had censured one of his men during this foray for trying to spare the life of an Indian child, reminding him that "nits become lice."

It was in this highly charged environment that Governor Evans wrote to Judge Castello one of many letters seeking his help with the Utes.

COLORADO SUPERINTENDENCY
INDIAN AFFAIRS

Denver, August 2, 1865

Hon. James Castello
Fair Play Park Co. C.T.

Dear Sir:
　　　Yours is received enclosing $90.00 as per agreement.
　　　As for "Colorado" [Chief Colorow] he left here in perfect friendship, and said he was satisfied. I gave him some shirts and also the man who came with him together with some light articles, the only things he could carry. Agent Head was here to distribute them and his interpreter "Ouray." The Major left to go ... the South Park, but I learn afterwards parted with "Colorado" and went to Conejos. This I presume is what he means by "vamoosing to Conejos." He and "Ouray" were professedly greatly pleased with my talk and the prospect of a distribution of one or two thousand sheep this fall and he wanted me to write to the people of Cash Creek that he was all right, which I did.
　　　I am astonished at your report and but for sickness, which kept me awake all night, I would come up in person

to see him.

 Will you go at the government expense and see him and give him - which you are hereby authorized to purchase --twenty sheep and a couple or three sacks of flour, or a couple beefs if you cannot get the sheep.

 Tell "Colorado" that I sent them to him because he could not take them, and assure him that I am not for the Mexicans to do any harm to the Indians, but will protect both; that I have ordered a great many sheep for them and will send him word to come, and get them near the Salt Works [in South Park] when the goods come which I hope for soon.

 I have ordered Major Head to go to see him immediately and to call upon you, and if it is all right when he comes, he can return. I trust I can rely upon your utmost efforts in this matter for which I will make suitable compensation.

Very Respectfully,
Your Obt. Servt.

Jno. Evans

Gov. & Ex. Officia
Supt. Ind. Affairs.

Chief Colorow was one of the most noted hostile Indian Chiefs in Colorado. He was labeled a "bully and a coward" commanding the "loathing and disrespect of both white man and Indian." Colorow and his band often threatened settlers, delighting in the terrified response he received by making gestures of scalping them. He was one of the few Utes who was belligerent in his assertions that whites did not belong in Indian territory, and gained a following of like-minded warriors. He gained further notoriety for a drunken altercation with Colorado Governor McCook in 1870, and then for leading a band of 50 Utes in defeating Major Thornburgh's nearly 200 troops after the White River [Meeker] Massacre in 1879. It is no small wonder that Governor Evans was relieved to have someone such as Judge Castello able to deal with

Colorow.

It became increasingly difficult for these early prospectors to remove the gold from its ore, and the thwarted miners began leaving the camps in droves. By 1865, Tarryall, Hamilton, Jefferson and Fairplay were almost ghost towns. Judge Castello decided that his future lay elsewhere than Fairplay. His son-in-laws had probably told him of the widely-used Ute Pass Wagon Road, and the lack of an adequate resting place for stagecoaches and teamsters. Chief Ouray and his other Ute friends had also probably told him of the importance of the crossroads at Twin Creek.

General Edward M. McCook became Governor of Colorado in 1869, and was quite open in his intentions of making a fast fortune. For a price, McCook furthered the business interests of railroads, mines, smelters, real estate and banks. One of his schemes toward this end revolved around Ouray's newly signed Hunt Treaty. In order to control the more than two hundred thousand dollar annual budget of this Treaty, McCook established the Denver Ute Agency. Under this arrangement, any Ute could register with Indian Agent James B. Thompson (McCook's brother-in-law) and receive his supplies and annuities in Denver. The East Oil Creek Trail (which loosely followed Teller Road #1 and Wildhorn) soon became a highly frequented Ute trail to Denver.

In June, 1870, Judge Castello and his son arrived in Twin Creek and began construction of a log cabin. He chose a site for this new home at the base of Fortification Hill, north of East Twin Creek. His home site was adjacent to the usual camping ground of his friend, Chief

Ouray. It was also propitiously located at the junction of the east-west Ute Trail Wagon Road and the north-south East Oil Creek Trail.

Catherine Castello and the children rejoined the Judge in November, and set up house keeping on that isolated ranch. The next nearest ranch was eleven miles west on the wagon road and belonged to Milton Pulver. Four other families joined the Castellos that fall: E.J. Smith at the South Platte crossing; the R. Marcott family; John Westal; and M. Riggs who settled south of Twin Creek on Four Mile Creek.

There was no doctor in the Florissant area until the 1880s. A feisty, independent woman whom the locals called "Dirty Woman" proffered her services as midwife and herbalist

ARTIST'S RENDERING OF JUDGE CASTELLO'S TRADING POST built in June 1870 near the junction of East Twin Creek and West Twin Creek, at the base of Fortification Hill.

NORTHERN UTE CHIEF, COLOROW, AND HIS BAND, circa 1875. Most of the warriors shown here were later involved in the White River Uprising in 1879. Top Row, L-R: Nicaagat (Captain Jack), Tanoa (Washington), Catz, Piah (Black Tailed Deer), Canalla (Johnson), Unknown. Bottom Row, L-R: Tabweah, Wanzits (Antelope), and Chief Colorow. *(Photo courtesy Colorado Historical Society)*

whenever needed. Nancy Ann Roberts (her given name) was a large, heavy-set woman who smoked a corn cob pipe and swore like a man. She defied convention at every opportunity, and consequently sported a bright red, sun-burned face through her refusal to wear a proper sunbonnet. She had thin, wispy hair which she twisted into a tiny knot on the top of her head. Her calico dress was always encrusted with a hefty layer of dirt and grime—which no doubt inspired her sobriquet. In addition to her nursing services, she owned and operated Dirty Woman Ranch and her own saw mill.

Social life for these early settlers was provided by seasonal outings for berry picking, spring and fall roundup, and by barn dances. For these occasions, the women spent an entire day in preparation—baking bread, assorted fruit pies, and cakes and frying chicken or roasting wild game. At dawn the next morning, large hampers of bread, pastries, meats, and preserves were loaded into the wagon along with assorted quilts and blankets, to be used both during the journey and for the usual overnight stay. Then the whole family piled into the farm wagon and the oxen slowly plodded their way to the destination. Once arrived, the children ran wildly as the adults mingled and exchanged the latest gossip and news. At mealtime, everyone shared their food, which was served accompanied by rich, thick campfire coffee or cool and aromatic wild mint tea.

Judge Castello's modest cabin was soon expanded to include a trading post, general store, and hostelry for overnight lodging. Travelers along the Ute Pass Wagon Road were thankful for the accommodations provided at the Castello Trading Post. Judge Castello was a "genial" man and a gracious host, and Catherine was famous for her hearty home cooking, especially her biscuits. Her table was always graced with her elegant silver and Bohemian glass casters, family heirlooms.

Anna Dickinson was one of these travelers. Anna was born into poverty in Philadelphia in 1842. However, she soon proved herself a child prodigy. She gained national recognition as a very popular anti-slavery lecturer when she was only 18. For many years, she averaged

AN 1800's SUNDAY AFTERNOON IN THE MOUNTAINS. These appear to be city folks, enjoying a picnic and some fishing, with a little target practice to spice it up. *(Photo courtesy Ute Pass Historical Society)*

EARLY SETTLERS PILE INTO THEIR FARM AND RANCH WAGONS for a gay afternoon of berry picking followed by a picnic. *(Photo courtesy Rose White)*

150 lectures, and earned approximately $20,000 a year! In September of 1873, she met up with Hayden's survey party and succeeded in climbing Long's Peak with Dr. Hayden. Anna then rode the Denver and Rio Grande down to Colorado Springs. Of course, she did this in style also—perched out front of the engine on the cow catcher! Of course, Pikes Peak had to be climbed before she headed west into South Park. (This was very much the same itinerary that Lady Isabella Bird would follow several months later.) Fortunately, Anna left a charming record of her travels up the Ute Pass Wagon Road. In her journal, *A Ragged Register*, (Published in 1879) Dickinson gives a vivid account of her stay at Castello's in Florissant.

[We] Got a pair of good beasties and comfortable vehicle, clambered into it cased in light woollen garments so that neither sunnings nor wettings could trouble us, with substantial hand-bags, a bucket to water the horses; some lunch; some field-glasses, and divers odds and ends by way of baggage—and made for the Twin Lakes and "Derry's."

Rode thirty-three miles the first day. From Colorado Springs to Manitou, up the wild Ute Pass to the beautiful open country beyond; through Hayden's [Divide] Pass, where on either side the road nature has piled a vast mass of boulders to the height of four hundred feet, as regularly and symmetrically as though done by a mason's hand; across land that was rich and prolific, though we had started at an elevation of six thousand and were unconsciously moving along to an elevation of nine thousand feet, and toward sun-setting turned a mile or so from the line of our travel to see some petrified stumps of trees.

And shall never forget the spot where they stood.

A place-like an enormous basin, the sides gently sloping up to the level brim all around. Short, soft gray grass covering the ground. Timber on the uplifted surrounding edge miles away, each twig and leaf of which stood out soft yet distinct as an ivory painting in one's hand. A sky and air for which I could find no likeness save the 'pearly clearness of the Celestial City," the coloring shot through it reflected from the clouds and the sunken sun making a 'light that never was on sea or land." The pallid massive stumps, ghostly and cold, of what had been wood ages before the deluge. Not a sound. Not a chirp of cricket, nor stir of twig or leaf, or blade of grass, nor whisper of bird. Not a sight or vestige of existence, human or brute. It was awful, yet filled with enchantment.

We carried its exalted spell till we reached Costello's [sic] jolly hospitable ranche, with its queer little rooms lined with canvas and adorned with innumerable copies of illustrated newspapers, its huge open fireplace made of petrified wood, its gorgeous fire, its royal supper, and yet more royal beds of sweet-smelling straw.

Don't you wish you knew Judge and Madame Costello, and that they would let you come to their ranche, and feed you and talk to you, and make you happy, and at departing allow you to capture from the museum on their open veranda some antelope-horns or deer-horns, or horns of Rocky Mountain sheep, mineral specimens or petrified wood?

If you don't, it is because you are a poor benighted mortal, with no knowledge of what you are rejecting.

We meandered away from it with reluctance, though we had before us some long heavenly days of driving across the South Park, and over the Arkansas Divide.

By 1873, Catherine Castello's seclusion in the Florissant Valley was lessened somewhat by the arrival of the Reverend David P. Long and his family. Reverend Long surveyed the valley, and decided to settle in the "petrified forest" since no one had yet laid claim to the area. He built a log cabin (just south of what would later become the Hornbek homestead) which had a magnificent view of Pike's Peak; he felt that it was the perfect homesite. Long planned to file a homestead claim as soon as the land was surveyed. His daughter, Atlanta (Long) Thompson,

Chapter V

wrote of these early days in Florissant in her autobiography, *Daughter of a Pioneer.*

When the few scattered settlers in the region heard that Pa was building a cabin and intended to live there, they came and helped him. This cabin was about eighteen feet long and fifteen feet wide. It was built of round logs and smaller logs were used for the roof. A large ridge pole was put across the logs when the walls were high enough and then smaller logs were laid on this ridge pole, forming the roof. These poles were usually covered with dirt, but Pa found some white clay near by, and he used this instead. This made a splendid covering for the roof until the three-day rains of August commenced and then it began to leak.

In one side of this cabin there was a small window. The only doorway was cut in one end and the door itself was made of rough boards with a wooden latch that fit down into a groove on the inside with a buckskin thong hanging on the outside. One could pull this thong and lift the latch. The latch string was always out. There were no locked doors in those days. In the other end of the room was a fireplace in which we burned pitch logs. One of these logs would burn all evening and throw out a cheery red glow. We children thought it great fun to throw pitch logs onto the fire. In addition to the fire place, there was a small cook stove in one corner of the room and in another corner were two or three shelves to hold some dishes. We had a home-made table and a few broken chairs which Pa had mended. There wasn't much room for furniture but we always had a trundle bed which could be pushed under the big bed in the daytime.

Pa could go out and kill a deer any day that we needed meat. The cotton-tail rabbits were plentiful, too, and we enjoyed them just as much as we did fried chicken. In this way we always had fresh meat.

Since there was no school for her children, Ma persuaded Pa to build on another room and she taught us children and the neighbor children, and even boarded one little girl who could not walk so far.

Chief Ouray and his Utes were still frequent visitors to the Florissant area all through this period, for it remained Tabeguache Ute hunting grounds in addition to being the crossroads for the East Oil Creek Trail and the Ute Pass Trail.

Atlanta (Long) Thompson wrote that "Chief Colorow was in our house many times. He was very friendly toward the white man. He could speak some English, and father enjoyed talking to him. Sometimes he would come and bring some of his tribe with him. They would sit on the floor and say, 'Heap pretty squaw,' meaning my mother, and then say, 'Me like heap biscuits.'"

REVEREND DAVID LONG AND HIS FAMILY, February 2, 1895. Long was the first white settler on what is now the Florissant Fossil Beds National Monument. This photo was taken three years after his wife Lydia died. Top Row (L-R): William, Eva, Rev. Long, Atlanta (Mrs. Silas Thompson). Bottom Row (L-R): Joseph, George, Emma, Loa. *(Photo courtesy Douglas & Virginia Pearce)*

Chapter V

In the winter of 1874-75, Chief Ouray camped near Florissant with a band of six hundred Utes. They remained there for several months, probably hunting, gathering herbs and berries, and trading with Castello. One day, a ranchman named J. Pleasant Marksbery—who lived along the Tarryall River—rode into town. He stopped at Castello's post office, tethered his horse, and went into the building. In the meantime, Ouray's War Chief, Shawano, recognized Marksbery's fine pony as one stolen from his Ute friend, Antelope. A Ute brave quickly removed the saddle and bridle, swung his leg across the pony's back, and rode off.

Agent Thompson (no relation to Atlanta Long Thompson) related what he recalled of the incident (over thirty years later) in his memoirs, *Sons of Colorado*, published in 1907.

> ...Marksberry [sic] went to the Ute camp, while the men were all out hunting, showed a paper which he said was an order from me as special agent, took the horse, and, with his boy leading the animal—he acting as rear guard—started for his home. Meantime Tab-We-Ap [Chief Tabernash, or Tabweah], coming in from the hunt, was told by his squaw what had occurred, and at once started in pursuit. All that could be ascertained from the boy, at the subsequent trial, was that he heard a shot, saw Marksberry fall from his horse, let fall the lariat by which he was leading the captured animal, and "streaked" it for home.
>
> Within a few hours the telegraph wires were burning again. The neighbors and friends of the murdered man gathered at Castello's, armed and frantic to attack the Ute camp. (They would have been wiped out in a few minutes.) However, the influence of dear old Judge Castello prevailed to keep them in check, and through his counsel they agreed to leave the settlement of the affair to the proper authorities.
>
> There is a homely saying, "Blessed is the man who bloweth his own bugle," etc. I will only blow mine to the extent of saying that, with the aid of Ouray, I succeeded in capturing the wicked

Tab-We-Ap, brought him to Denver, where he was confined in jail by order of the Commissioner of Indian Affairs, and every effort was made, and every opportunity offered the friends of Marksberry to convict him. No direct evidence was offered or produced, and after holding the prisoner for two months, the Commissioner of Indian Affairs at Washington ordered his release.

Tab-We-Ap was one of the party of "picnickers" that afterwards killed Jo. McLain near Deer Trail, and later was himself killed by Big Frank in the fight at Junction Ranch, in Middle Park.

Agent Thompson's account of Marksbery's murder appears to be seriously in error when it is compared with the contemporaneous newspaper accounts of the incident. *Rocky Mountain News* ran the following story on January 21, 1875.

THE MARKSBERY MURDER. Friday last J. Pleasant Marksbery, a well-known mountaineer, was shot and instantly killed by Shewano, the war chief, whose band are encamped near Mt. Pisgah, about 20 miles south of Florissant also south and west of Pikes Peak. The circumstances are about as follows: Last spring, during the deep snows at Colorado Springs, the Utes traded off some of their ponies. A Mr. Nat Colby purchased one for $20.00 and a revolver, but shortly afterward sold (?) it to Mr. Marksbery for a yoke of cattle. Marksbery had the pony in his possession until about the 20th (of December). Ouray's band of Utes were then camped near Judge Castello's ranch. Mr. Marksbery, who resided some sixteen miles from Florissant on Tarryall Creek, came to the place for letters, goods, etc., and while in the store some Utes stripped saddle and bridle off the pony, and rode off. Mr. Marksbery did not miss the pony until he was about ready to start home. He reentered the store where he was accused by Shawano of stealing the pony, which led to some rather harsh words between them. Marksbery, in the scuffle which ensued, got possession of Shawano's gun and told him he would keep it until his pony should be restored...

The Hunt Treaty of 1868 was very specific in its provisions for treatment of "bad men among the Indians." This Treaty states that such men will "deliver up the wrongdoer to the United States" once proof has been made to their Indian agent. In a follow up story printed in the *Rocky Mountain News* on January 26, 1875, further light is shed upon the murder.

THE MARKSBERY MURDER. Promptly in response to telegraphic order from the Indian department at Washington, Major Thompson a few days ago dispatched Chas. A. Jockmus to Florissant with orders to bring to Denver the Ute Indian Tabweah, who is charged with the Murder of Marksbery. On arriving at the Ute camp, Ouray willingly complied with Major Thompson's order and at once surrendered Tabweah. The party arrived here last evening when Tabweah was turned to the custody of Deputy Sheriff D.J. Cook and lodged in the County jail. John Ward came up as an interpreter, as also did Antelope who claims that the killing of Marksbery was done in self-defense. Ouray states that when Marksbery entered the Ute camp in search of the pony said to have been stolen he claimed that he had an order from Major Thompson and one from Ouray as well, for the delivery of the pony, which was not true; that after Marksbery rode away with the pony he was followed by Tabweah and another Indian who tried to induce Marksbery to surrender the animal, that he refused, and made frequent threatening demonstrations with his rifle, the result of which was that Tabweah fired upon him in self-defense and killed him.

UTE WARRIOR TABWEAH, ACCUSED OF KILLING MARKSBERY. Tabweah was killed in 1878 in an altercation with white settlers in Middle Park. He and forty Utes led by Piah and Washington tried to reclaim a meadow that they contended Ouray had no right to give away in treaties. Big Frank Addison shot him, and he was hastily buried in a shallow grave near Junction Ranch in Middle Park. *(Sketch from 1879 "Harper's Weekly")*

Clearly, the Shining Mountains of Colorado were not yet tamed, despite the number of new "civilized" inhabitants. They were certainly not the place for a genteel, lone woman to plan a horseback sightseeing excursion. However, that is precisely what Lady Isabella Bird decided to do in the winter of 1873. She was no novice at world travel, having begun exploring from her native England when she was but 20 years old. She had already visited Scotland, Hawaii, Canada, and the eastern United States before she reached the Rocky Mountains.

LADY ISABELLA BIRD AND BIRDIE. *(Illustration from the 1882 "A Lady's Life in the Rocky Mountains")*

Bird was 42 when she arrived at Greeley and rented a wiry little bay mustang pony, Birdie, who was to become her sole companion. Bird and Birdie set out, alone, in October 1873. Their 800 mile adventure carried them from Long's Peak, down the Goodnight-Loving Trail (Interstate 25) to Colorado Springs, west through Ute Pass and into Florissant, then north through South Park to Fairplay before heading east again. She arrived in Denver in December 1873. Bird kept a record of her travels in a series of letters, which were later published. In this volume, *A Lady's Life in the Rocky Mountains*, Bird gives a colorful description of her stop in

Florissant.

> ...I came upon wild pine forests [probably Florissant Canyon] with huge masses of rock from 100 to 700 feet high, cast here and there among them; beyond these pine-sprinkled grass hills, these, in their turn were bounded by interminable ranges, ghastly in the lurid evening, with the Spanish Peaks [Sangre de Cristos] quite clear, and the colossal summit of Mount Lincoln, the King of the Rocky Mountains, distinctly visible, though seventy miles away. It seemed awful to be alone on that ghastly ridge, surrounded by interminable mountains in the deep snow knowing that a party of thirty had been lost here a month ago. Just at nightfall the descent of a steep hill took me out of the forest and upon a clean log cabin, where, finding that the proper halting place [Castello's hotel] was two miles farther on, I remained. A truly pleasing, superior-looking woman [probably Lydia Long, Atlanta Long Thompson's mother] placed me in a rocking-chair; would not let me help her otherwise than by rocking the cradle, and made me "feel at home." The room, though it serves them and their two children for kitchen, parlour, and bedroom is the pattern of brightness, cleanliness, and comfort. At supper there were canned raspberries, rolls, butter, tea, venison, and fried rabbit, and at seven I went to bed in a carpeted log room, with a thick featherbed on a mattress, sheets, ruffled pillow slips, and a pile of warm white blankets.

Among her harrowing experiences, Bird tells of traveling through snow as high as

Birdie's back, and of weather so cold that ice crusted one of her own eyes closed. However,

her adventures in Colorado's Rockies seems only to have whetted her appetite, and she followed

it with travels to Japan, India, Tibet, China, Korea, and Persia. She finally made a home in

Scotland where she died at the ripe old age of 73.

Bird and Dickinson were not the only tourists visiting Florissant during the early 1870s. The *Centennial*, a newspaper published out of Georgetown (just west of Denver) reported on the several tourist sites at Florissant in 1876.

> FLORISSANT, in El Paso County, 35 miles west of Colorado Springs, is celebrated for the great variety and abundance of geological and mineralogical specimens found in its vicinity; and it has become a noted resort for tourists passing through that portion of the Territory.

An earlier *Centennial* article in February of that year asserted that "many" thousands of pounds of crystals had been removed from the Crystal Mountains (Topaz Butte/Crystal Peak) located about eight miles north of Florissant. This article reported that "last summer and fall there were from 25 to 30 miners here constantly, beside some thousands of tourists and excursionists." A large rectangular prism, measuring 6 inches at the base, and 18 inches long, was supposedly found in the area. Among these crystals were found Smoky Quartz, Adularia, Green, Purple and White Fleur Spar. These were the sacred stones of the Ute, their "wotai." In addition to these minerals, the article also expounded on the fascinating petrified stumps and fossilized remains at the "Petrified Stumps."

Another of the early and prominent settlers in the Florissant Valley was the Welty family. In 1871 Levi Welty and his three boys rode up Ute Pass and across the hills to Castello's trading post. When they asked about ranch land, the Judge directed them eighteen miles south, toward the Cripple Creek area. Welty took the Judge's advice, and soon had a prosperous ranch in the very valley that would later be platted as the town of Cripple Creek—the world's greatest gold camp. In fact, it was the Weltys who gave the little stream coursing through their ranch lands the name of "Cripple Creek" after two cowboys and a cow were injured there all in the same day.

Judge Castello found it easy to began a ranching enterprise at his newly established home on Twin Creek. Many of the travelers up the Ute Pass Wagon Road arrived with lame or foot-sore horses and oxen. These were easily traded, usually three or four jaded animals in exchange for one healthy animal. Within a few weeks, the investment paid its dividends as the mineral-rich grasses and pure mountain air quickly restored the vigor of the tired animals. And there was no shortage of the life-giving grass, as "vast acres of waving grass were visible" from the Castello's door.

Judge Castello soon added a second cabin, which was used as country store and trading post. Castello's trading post would have carried the staples common to pioneer life—flour; coarsely ground corn meal; coffee; dried apples, apricots and peaches; dried onions, squash and chili peppers; Mexican *piloncillos* (sugar squares); salted pork and salt. For his trade with the Indians, the Judge would have lined the walls of the Trading Post with Navajo blankets, bolts of calico, and rifles. Iron cooking pots, strings of red chili, and bundles of crude tallow candles would hang from the rafters, as well as various pieces of harness and tack. Brightly colored glass beads would mingle with boxes of powder and shells along rough-hewn log counters.

Travelers were pressed into service as mail carriers until 1872, when Judge Castello established a post office. He named his post office Florissant after his home town of Florissant, Missouri. The little community of Twin Creek was now officially "Florissant." Fred Smith soon established a much-needed blacksmith shop within a block of the Trading Post, and thus the seeds were planted for a small town. By 1876 the population of Florissant had increased to approximately seventy residents, living in twenty-two log houses. There was now a small log schoolhouse and three sawmills. However, ranching remained the principal commercial activity in the area.

Samuel Hartsell had set the standard for ranching west of Pikes Peak when he established a 9,000 acre ranch at the fork of the South Platte and Fairplay branch of the Platte in 1863. He gained his place in history by bringing the first pedigreed short-horn cattle (an English breed) into Colorado. Hartsell also built a small community around his ranch, with a hotel at the Hot Springs, a school house, wagon and blacksmith shops and a saw mill.

To be a really large Colorado cattle baron, however, it seemed that one should be named John Wesley. Colorado's two preeminent cattle growers were John Wesley Iliff, who ran 25,000 head on the plains east of Denver ; and John Wesley Prowers, who ran 10,000 head on the Arkansas east of La Junta.

Iliff began buying longhorns from a Texan named Charlie Goodnight in 1866 and crossing them with his shorthorn Illinois bulls. He was able to quadruple his investment on each cow, and the two entered a very lucrative partnership. Goodnight, and his Texas partner Oliver Loving, blazed a cattle trail from Texas, up through Denver, to Wyoming (along present-day Interstate 25). Between 1866 and 1884 they moved over five million longhorn cattle over what was called the Goodnight-Loving cattle trail. Charlie Goodnight finally moved all of his ranching operations to Colorado in 1869. He bought a large parcel—a third of the Nolan Land Grant—just west of Pueblo and became a prominent business man in that town.

Ranching in Colorado was becoming big business. Hungry miners, as well as homesteaders and the new city dwellers, created a thriving market for beef. In 1867, Colorado's ranchers organized the Colorado Stock Growers Association in order to begin recording brands. Branding was critical in establishing ownership of the cattle herds that mingled on the open range land. Colorado had virtually unlimited open grazing until the advent of barbed wire in Colorado in the late 1870s. Until then, however, the homesteaders in the Florissant area had to build picket fences or log fences around their homes and precious kitchen gardens in order to keep the cattle out. The Florissant school had a charming three-rail fence in order to keep the cattle from tramping over the children at play. Area ranchers held cooperative roundups each spring and fall in order to sort their respective stock for branding and shipping.

When the Castellos first settled in Florissant, there were only a handful of other communities within the entire state. The closest, of course, was Colorado City (formerly El Paso), at the base of Ute Pass, which was founded about 1859. About sixty miles south of Colorado City, a handful of Mountain Men had established a small fort "El Pueblo" in 1841, but were all murdered by angry Utes in 1854. The gold fever of 1859 was key to reviving the settlement, however, as well as to giving birth to Canon City located another fifty miles west.

All of these early towns were propitiously located along the major roads leading to the gold strikes. In addition to these towns, the gold strikes also gave birth to a number of short-lived communities—Tarryall, Fairplay, Hamilton, and Jefferson, to name a few (although Fairplay and Jefferson were later revived). With few exceptions, the towns that were established to serve travelers enjoyed longer lives and a more steady prosperity than those playing host to the gold seekers. There was greater stability, and less risk, in supplying food, clothing, transportation and other services than in challenging the stubborn earth to release her precious minerals.

A year after Judge Castello established his trading post on the banks of Twin Creek, General William J. Palmer was struck by the beauty of Pikes Peak and platted his Fountain Colony—now called Colorado Springs. He began construction immediately on his grand vision of an intercontinental, north-south railroad. By 1872, the tracks of his narrow-gauge Denver and Rio Grande Railroad had reached Pueblo from Denver, pausing momentarily before snaking their way down through New Mexico and further up the Arkansas River on a detour to Colorado's gold camps.

In the midst of the national financial panic of 1873, General Palmer and his business partners became justifiably anxious about their ability to sell the town lots in Fountain Colony. Palmer's financial backer, the Englishman William Blackmore, had formed a fortuitous relationship with the new chief of the U.S. Geological and Geographical Survey, Dr. Ferdinand V. Hayden. Hayden and Blackmore had met in Laramie, Wyoming, in 1868 while Hayden was working on his famous survey of the Nebraska Territory and Blackmore was consulting with officials of the Union Pacific Railroad. Blackmore and Palmer were considering the purchase of the vast Sangre de Cristo Land Grant, and enlisted Hayden to do a resource survey of the area. Hayden spent the next several months traveling through the grant area in Northern New Mexico and Colorado's San Luis Valley, assessing its potential. He then submitted a five page report to Blackmore. In 1869, Blackmore published Hayden's report in London in a promotional book titled *Colorado: Its Resources, Parks, and Prospects.*

Blackmore later accompanied (and helped finance) Hayden's famous second survey of Yellowstone in 1872. Tragically, however, Blackmore's lovely young wife died of "fatigue" during this survey. Publication of this survey, which included breathtaking photos by William Henry Jackson and ethereal paintings by Thomas Moran, resulted in the creation of Yellowstone Park in 1872.

Blackmore felt that Hayden could generate as much excitement about Colorado as he had for Yellowstone with one of his surveys. He also convinced Hayden to include an assessment of his coal fields near Trinidad and Raton. Hayden agreed to this plan, and convinced Congress to finance a similar survey of Colorado beginning in September, 1873, complete with Blackmore's coal fields. Hayden then had his second-in-command, James T. Gardner, publish the results in a *Report Upon the Southern Coal and Iron Fields Of Colorado Territory.* When this report came to light, it caused a small scandal. It solely benefited Palmer and Blackmore's land holdings in that area, but was financed by the United States Congress. Fortunately, however, the remainder of the Hayden's survey benefited all of Colorado.

Hayden was an ex-professor and ex-doctor who found his calling as a geologist and paleontologist in the far reaches of the unknown West. He was a slightly built man with an enormous dark, bushy beard and mustache. He had a penchant for dressing oddly, usually sporting a weather beaten frock coat and ever present leather pouch filled with stones. The Sioux Indians had long before christened him "He Who Picks Up Stones Running" because of his habit of constantly jumping off his horse and gathering rocks along the way.

Dr. A.C. Peale–a former student of Hayden's and a noted mineralogist–accompanied Hayden on his Colorado survey. In 1874, he recognized and documented the scientific importance of the "Petrified Forest." He presented his specimens to the famous paleobotanist, Leo Lesquereux, who determined that Florissant's fossils were approximately 40 million years old.

Hayden spent the summers of 1873, 1874, and 1875 directing his highly trained, youthful parties of about twenty men each in the daunting task of mapping the Colorado Rockies. Hayden's gang also spent a good deal of time at Ben Requa's general store and restaurant in Fountain, Colorado. It was there in 1873 that the erstwhile cowboy Bob Womack met Hayden. Hayden quizzed Womack about the mountains and meadows on the west slope of Pikes Peak, which was their present objective. Womack directed the survey team up Ute Pass to Florissant, then south down the trail to the Welty Ranch. One of Hayden's base camps, about twenty-seven miles west of Colorado Springs on the Ute Pass Wagon Road, was later named Hayden's Divide (now called simply "Divide"). When Hayden's team visited the Cripple Creek area a week later, they discovered a large volcanic formation of "trachorheite."

One of the surveyors, H.T. Wood, returned to the area in 1874, convinced that the trachorheite held gold-bearing ore. He formed a partnership, and dug a hundred foot tunnel, which he named the Lone Tree Prospect Tunnel. Womack watched and listened to all this activity, gaining the knowledge that enabled him to make his famous discovery of Cripple Creek gold in 1890. Wood was not so fortunate, however. He and his partners abandoned their site after finding a worthless "white iron"—which was very probably sylvanite, Cripple Creek's characteristic gold ore.

Hayden made a practice of meeting with the local settlers in each region, and strictly adhering to the place names that were currently in use. Many of these names have, however, changed in the intervening years. Hayden's maps, for instance, show "Topaz Butte" rather than Crystal Peak; Witcher Creek is labeled "West Twin Creek;" Four Mile Creek is "West Oil Creek;" Hay Creek is "East Oil Creek;" Woodland Park is simply "Junction;" and Lake George is "Links Ranche."

Hayden's survey was an unequalled success, and was greatly responsible for Congress' decision to make Colorado a state in 1876. Unfortunately, the selling of Colorado came too late for Palmer and Blackmore. In 1877 Palmer defaulted on the Denver and Rio Grande bonds that

Blackmore had so avidly sold to his friends. Sickened by this failure, Blackmore became a hopeless alcoholic and ended by committing suicide in England. Palmer, of course, went on to make other fortunes with his town and his railroad. Florissant, however, received a new lease on life now that the area had been properly surveyed. The Homestead Act of 1862 stated that:

> ... any citizen, or person with intention of becoming a citizen, who was the head of a family and over twenty-one years of age, could become possessed of 160 acres of the surveyed public domain after five years of continuous residence on his tract and the payment of a small ($26 to $34) registration fee. If the homesteader desired, the title could actually pass into his hands after six months residence and the payment of the minimum price of $1.25 per acre.

TYPICAL CAMP SCENE OF HAYDEN'S SURVEY PARTY. (L-R) William H. Jackson (photographer), Dr. A.C. Peale, G.P. Dixon, and Dr. Turnbull. It was Peale who first recognized the scientific importance of the fossils he found in the Florissant Valley while a member of Hayden's 1873 survey. *(Photo courtesy USGS)*

BOB WOMACK, THE ERSTWHILE COWBOY, led Hayden's survey party to Pikes Peak backcountry.

They, in turn, tutored him on the geological aspects of gold ore. He was an apt student, later discovering the great gold

camp of Cripple Creek. *(Photo courtesy Colorado Springs Pioneers Museum)*

Chapter V

CHAPTER VI: HOMESTEADING IN THE

FLORISSANT VALLEY

Within the mysterious circle of life, birth and death closely follow one another in endless succession—much as summer always follows winter. Each cloud threatens a storm and promises a rainbow. In its embryonic state, the little town of Florissant was not immune to these cycles of life.

First, the much beloved old Judge Castello died in the spring of 1878. The *Rocky Mountain News* carried his obituary, noting that "the state [of Colorado], and especially his county, have lost a most worthy and useful citizen, and a wide circle of personal friends will mourn with his stricken family in their great bereavement." Close on the heels of the Judge's death, a terrible drought struck the entire state of Colorado, devastating farmers and ranchers alike. Lightning struck the crisp, lifeless grasses and the dry, brittle trees, sending forest fires blazing all over the state. Smoke from the fires on Pikes Peak obliterated its snow-shrouded summit, and filled the lungs of the mountain settlers as well as those of the wealthy new land owners in Palmer's Fountain City.

As the earth humbled her people with these natural disasters, she also grudgingly yielded more of her riches. Silver had been found in Leadville, and it soon became the world's largest silver camp. Gold was discovered in Aspen, and the newly discovered mines in Telluride held increasing promise. Wave after wave of obsessed prospectors engulfed the Shining Mountains— the sacred Ute hunting grounds, assured as theirs "forever" in treaty after treaty.

Silver was the money of the land. Any miner with a pick, a shovel and a will to work could quickly fill his pockets. Silver was now worth $1.29 per ounce, and during this period, wages of $1.00 per day were the standard. With a little sweat, a miner could easily dig the equivalent of a month's wages in one day or less. Once it was removed from the ground, the silver was readily converted to cash at the numerous smelters springing up around the state. There were now smelters at Pueblo, Denver, Leadville, Durango, Salida, Silverton, Telluride and Lake City. Colorado's mountains were "the stuff that dreams were made of"—but the Utes were a problem.

Why should these few Indians own such vast stretches of Colorado's mountains and wealth? They didn't even value the riches beneath their feet and, in fact, felt that the whites were stabbing their Mother Earth in her face with each stroke of a miner's pick. Indeed, they felt that ripping into Mother Earth for her minerals was much the same as ripping open the belly of one's own mother in order to feed oneself. When Colorado's ancient volcanoes erupted, creating vast mineral deposits, they also fomented the later conflict between the two cultures, white and red.

Colorado's Utes were a peaceable people, more inclined to cohabitation than to confrontation, and this posed an ethical dilemma for their covetous white neighbors. The *Denver*

Tribune sought to remedy this untenable situation by beginning a "Utes Must Go" campaign. The paper was soon filled with slanted stories of Ute misconduct, even attributing the numerous forest fires to the Ute. The paper neglected to point out that Colorado was in the midst of a drought, and that lightning was the most common cause of all the fires.

Tensions between the settlers and the Utes began to mount, and finally ignited a fatal conflagration at the White River Ute Agency in northwest Colorado. Senator Henry Teller, one of the staunchest opponents of the Ute presence, appointed reformist Nathan Meeker as Indian Agent at White River. Meeker's rigid management style, and his overbearing efforts to transform his nomadic charges into sedentary farmers, propelled him along a tragic path. When he finally threatened to shoot all of their ponies, the Utes rebelled, killing Meeker and ten of his men. (This tragic incident was related in greater detail in Chapter 3.)

This was exactly the catalyst that the *Denver Tribune* needed. The "Utes Must Go!" campaign now echoed throughout Colorado, and the United States Congress soon responded to its pressure. The small band of angry White River Utes had succeeded in undoing all that had been gained from over 200 years of treaties and peaceful cohabitation. In 1881, Col. McKenzie herded thousands of Ute exiles to newly created reservations in southern Colorado and eastern Utah. No longer would Ute warriors seek guidance from the Great Spirit in Vision Quests on the slopes of Pikes Peak, where their people were created. No longer would sick or troubled Utes bathe in the healing mineral waters at Manitou Springs. No longer would Ute medicine men gather sacred healing stones on the slopes of the Crystal Mountains. No longer would the

Ute hunt the elk and the deer and the antelope in their ancient hunting grounds.

A flood of eager new homesteaders followed close on the heels of the Utes' departure. However, this flood was preceded by a modest first wave of homesteaders in 1877. They came after the publication of Hayden's *Atlas*. For Hayden had not only delineated the probabilities of Colorado's mineral wealth, but also its suitability for farming and ranching. An added bonus to Hayden's surveys was that the land could now be legally homesteaded. It is interesting that the Act does not discriminate by either gender or race. This lack of discrimination proved to be the lure in attracting another of Florissant's more famous settlers—Adeline Hornbek.

Adeline was born in the Year of the Shooting Stars, 1833—the same year that the Ute chief Ouray was born. Her brother, Alexander, had become an Indian trader on the Creek land that is now Oklahoma. Adeline met and fell in love with his friend and fellow trader, Simon A. Harker. They married and settled in Oklahoma for a while. However, Simon was seized with bad health shortly thereafter which he attributed to exposing himself to bad weather while out buying cattle. This lingering illness, and the coming Civil War, probably motivated the Harkers to move to Colorado. Adeline, Simon and their two infant children, Frank and Annie, made the trip across the arid plains by ox-drawn wagon. She was only 27 when she and Simon settled on Cherry Creek, just east of Denver. Here they established a cattle ranch in 1861, and began a forty year ranching odyssey for Adeline.

In addition to ranching, Simon also served as Indian Agent for the newly founded Colorado Territory. Raising beef for hungry miners and employing diplomatic skills with Native

Americans was a major cultural transition for Harker, who had emigrated from England when he was only 13. The family seemed to prosper, however, and engaged in a number of real estate transactions in the area. A second son, George, was born in 1863. Simon became a member of the Masonic Order, and was also active in the Republican Party.

Another of the gold-seekers of 1859, Dr. George M. Willing, provides a rare glimpse of Denver at this time in his diary, published by the *Daily Missouri Republican* on August 9, 1859.

> Denver City and Auraria together make up but an inconsiderable village, with Cherry Creek--when there's any water in it--running through the middle of it. There are here about one hundred and fifty houses, with about forty lodges of the Arrapahoe [sic] Indians --quite a number of negro women, with a pleasant but scanty sprinkling of white ones, and a mixed male population of white, black, red, and yellow.

Dr. Willing's fellow traveler, William Magill, wrote to his sister in Florissant, Missouri, in June of that same year that he had "not seen or heard anything of the Florissant Boys [Castello's?] with the exception of Henry Haner...We suppose that they are all in the mountains."

It may have been during this period that the Harkers met another Indian Agent, Judge James Castello of Fairplay. Historians have not yet documented when these two families met. However, the Castello's were to become friends and neighbors of Adeline when she later moved to Florissant. Colorado's Indian Agents were a small but elite group, and it is very possible that this group provided the connection with Castello that would later draw Adeline into the Florissant Valley. It is also possible that Judge Castello and Simon Harker met through their mutual involvement in Colorado's Republican Party.

Heavy snows in 1864 kept the Utes from a successful winter buffalo hunt, causing them great distress and starvation. When these same high mountain snows melted in the spring, they caused a devastating flood along Cherry Creek. Its roiling waters destroyed the tranquil pastoral life of the Harkers as they washed through their home and over their pastures. The financial losses were too much for Simon and he died shortly thereafter, though he was only 39. Adeline was left to rebuild her ranch and her life while caring for her three children, aged from 1 to 5. She seems to have managed very well, and was actually able to purchase their 80-acre Cherry Creek homestead in 1866.

A few months later, the red-haired, 31-year-old Adeline married Elliot D. Hornbek in Denver. Four years later she bore him a son, and also named him Elliot. This marriage was brief and ill-fated, however, and Adeline was abandoned by Hornbek around 1875. She and her three boys, now aged 16, 12, and 5, and Annie, now 15, continued in the family tradition of ranching. Fortunately for them, two Texans, Charlie Goodnight and Oliver Loving, had forged a major cattle trail up from Texas, through Denver and on into Wyoming. (Their cattle Trail loosely follows the path of present day I-25.) The demand for beef was so great that over five million head of cattle were moved over this trail between 1866 and 1884.

Adeline's second son, George Harker, recalls that his mother and brothers moved to Florissant in 1876. This complements the oral tradition of Rev. David Long's family, which maintains that Rev. Long's brother-in-law, Frank Sens, sold their ranch to the Hornbeks. Frank had been given custody of the property while Rev. Long took his family on an ill-fated sabbatical to live at the new Mormon colony in Utah in 1874. At odds with this account, however, is the Homestead Proof form filed by Adam Hill in 1880. In it he claims that he purchased a shell of a house and some fencing from Frank "Sence" in 1874. Hill's homestead lies adjacent to Adeline's on the south.

ADELINE HORNBEK, A SINGLE MOTHER WITH TRUE GRIT. Widowed by her first husband, and abandoned by her second, Adeline homesteaded in the Florissant Valley around 1876. *(Photo courtesy Hornbek/Stone Family)*

HORNBEK HOMESTEAD, AS RESTORED. Adeline and her four children built this lovely homestead and successfully ranched in the Florissant Valley for over 20 years. Her homestead is now listed on the National Register of Historic Places. *(Photo courtesy of the Florissant Fossil Beds National Monument)*

The first documented evidence of the Hornbek presence, however, is Adeline's homestead application of 1878. Adeline's homestead site lies about one mile south of present-day Florissant on Teller County Road #1, within the boundaries of the Florissant Fossil Beds National Monument.

Nothing remains of the Long ranch, unfortunately. This is probably because it was built of "round logs." These tend to crack in the cool, dry mountain air and then to fill with rain and snow. The alternate filling, freezing, and further cracking soon reduce the logs to a hollow collection of sawdust and wood pulp. What was left of the Long's modest Petrified Forest cabin was probably recycled into fence posts to keep the cattle from Adeline's garden. It is truly remarkable that Adeline, a single mother, had the means to build such a lovely home by herself. No doubt, all of the ranchers and homesteaders in the area turned out in pioneer style for a "barn raising" for Adeline. Atlanta (Long) Thompson wrote that this was the usual method of building a home in the area.

Adeline's new home was one and a half stories with a pine shingle roof. There were three bedrooms upstairs and one downstairs, a kitchen with baking nook, and a parlor. Her compound boasted a barn, which stabled nine horses and had an attached wagon shed. Adeline also built a milk house, chicken house and a large corral for her livestock. In the beginning, she cultivated only three acres, producing some hay and potatoes, as well as her garden vegetables. There were about seventy other residents in the area at this time, and they undoubtedly helped the young widow to build her new home.

Adeline's son, George Harker, recalled an alarming incident with the notorious Ute Chief Colorow in a 1937 interview with the *Gazette Telegraph*.

> As a youth [in 1878 when he was fifteen years old] he had a fear of Indians and he said ... that as some came near the house, and one started to walk to the house, he got the loaded gun and stood at defense at the door. The wily old Indian chief [Colorow] upon being asked into the house quickly sensed what had almost happened and remarked: "White boy very white. Heap scared."

FRANK F. CASTELLO, circa 1900. Frank's father, Judge James Castello, founded Florissant in 1870. Frank transformed the Judge's rustic Ute Trading Post into the prosperous Florissant Mercantile which he sold to William C. Allen around 1898. *(Photo courtesy Leo & Julia Kimmett)*

There was a small log school house about a mile from Adeline's homestead, and the boys probably joined the other children of the area in walking to school each day. School records show that Adeline was secretary of the School District in 1880. When Judge Castello died in 1878, his son Frank took over the trading post and soon developed it into the Florissant Mercantile. Adeline ran the Mercantile in 1883 while Frank spent a year and a half prospecting

FRANK CASTELLO'S MERCANTILE, circa 1886. The building on the right, and sharing a wall, is McLaughlin & Horrigan's Drug Store. The building on the far right is the McLaughlin home, which still graces the corner of Highway 24 and Teller County Road #31. *(Photo courtesy Pikes Peak Library District)*

for gold in the San Juan Mountains north of Durango.

Ute Pass Wagon Road was heavily traveled during this period, as it was the only road to the gold fields that wasn't a toll road, and Frank Castello's Florissant Mercantile prospered. Florissant's population began to grow steadily and in 1876 the Prussian Count Louis Otto de Pourtales also homesteaded just north of Florissant. He was soon joined by his sister Berthe, an international beauty.

Countess Berthe had come to Cambridge to join her father, the Count Louis Frances de

Pourtales, a scientist at Harvard. He had emigrated from France in 1847 to join the Geodetic Survey in Washington, D.C., but later moved to Boston. When she was "hardly more than a child," the slender, blonde Countess Berthe entered into a tragic marriage with the very wealthy Sebastian Schlesinger. Berthe and Sebastian had two small daughters before deciding to divorce. She sought to mend her broken heart by accepting her brother's invitation to visit him at his ranch in Florissant in the early 1880s.

Berthe often traveled down the Ute Pass Wagon Road to Colorado Springs, where she was befriended by society matron, Frances Metcalfe Bass. Berthe was tall and gracious, with a knowledge of several languages, and was considered one of the loveliest women of her day.

Frances Bass later described Berthe at this time as appearing in the Springs "closely veiled, wearing a red cloak tightly buttoned about her throat, with a gray fur collar. She came there broken in health and sad of heart, seeking strength. She had gone first to the Adirondacks with her daughters, where of turkey red calico, she made them dresses—cheap dresses—that were the envy of all campers."

Berthe's cousin, Count James Pourtales, left his vast estates in Prussia to follow her to Colorado in 1884. He had been smitten by Berthe's beauty, and determined to make her his wife. Count James was a tall and imposing man, well over six feet. He had a large black beard, constantly smoked a pipe, and was followed everywhere he went by a brace of devoted dachshunds. He was considered a "good fellow" on account of his never-failing good humor.

SUNDAY AFTERNOON OUTING, 1880s STYLE. Burros were the preferred mode of transportation in the mountains. They were stronger and more sure-footed than horses. *(Photo courtesy Ute Pass Historical Society)*

Count James had been an intimate of Chancellor Bismarck, and easily fit in with the society of Colorado Spring's "Little London." His mother had been a German princess, and was the toast of Paris at the Court of Empress Eugenie. In the midst of wooing his cousin Berthe, Count James also was taken by the beauty of a failing Colorado Springs dairy farm, the Broadmoor. The Count bought the 1600-acre farm and implemented numerous reforms in an attempt to make it a profitable enterprise.

He steadily increased his land holdings, and is credited with being one of the earliest settlers to understand the importance of water rights. He bought 250 acres of nearby ranch land, irrigation ditches and water rights from the Rose Brothers. He then built Cheyenne Lake, and endured a constant feud with prairie dogs to keep them from burrowing into the dam and draining the lake. In a further scheme to enhance his profits, he platted Broadmoor City, then dreamed up a fancy European-style Casino as an added attraction. He and the Countess Berthe were eventually married and became the cream of Springs society.

In the meantime, Berthe's brother, Count Louis Otto de Pourtales, was also making a reputation for himself. He homesteaded a section of land about four miles north of Florissant and begin building a credible ranch of his own. Frances Bass writes that he was a good "horseman and dancer, born lover, he carried a guitar on which he picked a few chords, singing a monotonous tale of unrequited passion as persistently melancholy as the call of a mourning dove." He became somewhat notorious over his infatuation with Queen Palmer, General Palmer's young and beautiful wife. He often rode down to Palmer's palatial home in Glen Eyrie to sing his melancholy love songs under Queen's window. Frances Bass and her friends dubbed him the "Mute Seraph"—perhaps for his manner of quietly hovering around any beautiful woman.

Frances Bass writes that her Mute Seraph once threatened suicide after being rejected by another of his unrequited loves, "Little Peaches." His heart seems to have staunchly rebounded at each of these devastating blows, however, for he eventually married and settled down. In August, 1881, the hopelessly romantic Count Louis Otto deeded the ownership of his Florissant ranch to his new bride, Laura Mary Montgomery, for "one dollar and the consideration of love and affection."

Count Pourtales built a beautiful log home on his 320 acre ranch, and ran fancy imported German cattle on the surrounding open range. His eye for beauty and grace did not fail him in siting his home—it claimed a breathtaking view of Pikes Peak to the southeast as well as an imposing view of Crystal Peak to the west. His bride, Countess Laura, later delighted in regaling her grandchildren with stories of her life at the ranch. It seems that most of Little London's society traveled up the Ute Pass to attend the fancy balls at the ranch house with its Parisian wallpapers and expensive appointments.

Her sister-in-law, the beautiful Countess Berthe, always created a stir with her visits, arriving in a fancy carriage, elegantly dressed and accompanied by an entourage of assorted dogs straining at their leashes.

A favorite family story centers on the fortunes of a hapless young Lord from England. Frances Bass writes of these unfortunate gentlemen in her memoirs *Heritage of Years.*

> [These] Younger sons [who did not inherit] came from England with Anglo-Saxon land-hunger, equipped with the best of saddles, shotguns and rifles, and coin enough to pay their way. Unfortunately, many had a taste of life en route, and arrived penniless, with their belongings in pawn in Kansas City, or some other hard town, having bucked the tiger in gambling houses. The heart's desire of all was to own a large ranch...

It seems that Count Louis Otto had made a friend of one such young Englishman. According to Countess Laura, this unfortunate young man had not only lost his fortune, but had fabricated glowing accounts of his "ranch" in letters to his family. Naturally, his proud parents were eager to visit this remarkable son and see his vast lands and cattle. The young man was in a delicate quandary, but Count Louis Otto came to his rescue. He and Laura planned a timely visit with friends in the Springs, allowing the English Lord to produce a charade for his parents at the Pourtales ranch in Florissant!

Unfortunately, Count Louis Otto also chose to use round-log construction for his beautiful home. Rain and frost have steadily worked on the logs for the last 100 years until their hollowed cores collapsed, sending the beautiful dormer windows crashing through the roofs of the kitchen and the parlor below. Remnants of the elegant cut granite fireplace lie scattered in a meadow of feathery blue flax. Only the extensive, well-built corrals have survived, giving silent testimony to the great care that Count Pourtales extended to his pure-bred cattle.

Another of the Count's neighbors, Frank Burnham, filed a homestead claim in 1875 about a mile west of Florissant on the Ute Pass Wagon Road. He found an old trapper's cabin there (perhaps left by Kit Carson's trappers) and lived in it while he built his large log homestead house. Some of the rough hewn beams measure almost two feet thick, and their sturdy presence even to this day gives mute testimony to the wisdom of squaring the logs. Burnham steadily added to his ranch over the next few years as members of his family filed on adjacent homesteads. He eventually accumulated over 500 acres for his Twin Creek Ranch. He added a small shed for saddles and harness, a bunkhouse for about twelve "waddies" or cowboys, and a carriage house.

COUNT LOUIS OTTO DE POURTALES, COUNTESS LAURA MONTGOMERY DE POURTALES,

AND THEIR DAUGHTER LOUIS BERTHE on her burro circa 1892. The barn in the background shows the same

self-destructing round-log construction as their baronial two-story log home. *(Photo courtesy Walts Collection, Florissant*

Heritage Foundation)

Adjacent to the western boundary of Twin Creek Ranch, John and Mary Wilson staked

a homestead claim in 1874. And adjacent to them on the north, Charles H. Sisler staked a

homestead. In the tradition of the "Florissant Boys," the Wilsons and their nine children also

came from Missouri in a covered wagon . Twin Creek's clear, meandering waters and grass-

filled meadows soon became home to the Wilson's cattle, too.

However, they chose to summer their stock in the cool, high valleys of Breckenridge.

CHILDREN RAISED ON RANCHES LEARNED TO BE COWBOYS AT A TENDER AGE. This youngster is getting a taste of bawling calves and burning hide during a roundup west of Florissant in 1895. *(Photo courtesy Ute Pass Historical Society)*

Calas, the oldest, inherited the lonely job of moving the lumbering animals across Wilkerson Pass, then along the Platte into South Park, turning north over Hoosier Pass into Breckenridge each spring. The long trek was reversed in the fall before the snows fell. Calas' progress was monitored by a herd of wild mustangs, led by an ethereal, prancing roan stallion with flaxen mane and tail. This Strawberry Roan was coveted by all the local ranchmen, but somehow always eluded capture.

Calas Wilson eventually left the lonely life of cow punching and opened a barber shop and a cafe in the blossoming town of Florissant. As Frank Castello's Mercantile prospered, Calas purchased a half interest and watched his investment steadily grow. He later married a lovely woman who had come to enjoy the beauty of the Florissant Valley on the Wildflower Train.

When gold was found in Cripple Creek, Calas was struck with gold fever. He fiendishly worked his claims, certain that untold wealth was just a day's work away. Vainly he tried to ignore the bitter cold of Cripple's winters, working his claims and sleeping in a flimsy tent. But he died of complications from pneumonia when he was only 39, leaving a young wife and four small children.

When Calas left the family ranch, his chores fell to his younger brother, George. He learned early to ride a bronc, rope a calf, brand cattle, build fences and all of the other ranching skills he would need for the rest of his life. George married an aristocratic young Englishwoman, Ada Plaisted, when he turned 29, and together they built up the family homestead over the next forty-three years.

Settlers in the Florissant area were soon provided with farm fresh milk and freshly churned butter when Richard and Mary Houghton homesteaded a dairy just a mile north of town in 1885. Houghton was a Civil War veteran, and took advantage of the special Homestead provisions accorded them. "Uncle Dick" became very active in community affairs, serving on the school board for a number of years. Residents of the area were no longer forced to build log homes, as the population was increased by J.F. Frizzell and Robert Berrs, who operated

GEORGE AND ADA ANN WILSON, who lived on the 1874 Wilson homestead a mile west of Florissant, adjacent to Burnham's (later Allen's) Twin Creek Ranch. *(Photo courtesy Rolland Wilson)*

sawmills. They were soon joined by a family of extremely skilled carpenters, the Allens. William P. Allen, the father, homesteaded about three miles southwest of Florissant at Big Spring Ranch, now home to Sanborn Western Camp. His son William chose a homestead site about a mile northwest of his father's, at the base of Blue Mountain, later adding a second section near Burnham's. His brother Silas chose a site adjacent to his father's on the south. Carpentry was the Allen family forte—they built the elegant Victorian-style Cliff House Hotel and skating rink in Manitou Springs, and then built the steps to Seven Falls in Cheyenne Canyon.

WILLIAM C. ALLEN'S LOVELY TWIN CREEK RANCH. The compound includes Thomas Burnham's 1872 log homestead/barn and outbuildings, and a trapper's cabin dating from the 1850s. The ranch is now listed on the National Register of Historic Places. *(Photo courtesy Harold & Celinda Kaelin)*

Young William undoubtedly led the family to the area, for he also worked as a stagecoach driver on the McLaughlin Line, carrying passengers along the Ute Trail Wagon Road to the gold fields. Florissant now had mail service three times each week, as the Concord stages were pressed into service hauling letters and packages.

Passengers were snugly tucked into the coach under buffalo lap robes. Four matched horses snorted in the cold morning air as they plodded along at five or six miles an hour. Fifteen miles up the Ute Pass Wagon Road, at Summit Park (now Woodland Park), the horses

WILLIAM P. ALLEN (FATHER OF WILLIAM C. AND SILAS) who homesteaded south of Florissant in 1883 at what is now Sanborn Western Camps. *(Photo courtesy Kathleen Cramer)*

were changed and the passengers were offered a light lunch. Back into the stage all would pile, as the fresh horses proceeded to pull their burden to the 9,165 foot crest of Ute Pass at Hayden's Divide. The coach then burned its brake as it rolled down the winding, boulder-lined slopes of Twin Rocks Road, arriving in Florissant in time for supper and an overnight stay. Early next morning, the stage would continue on its way, either due west on the South Park Road to Sam Hartsell's, or north from Links Ranche (Lake George) up the Hamilton Road to Tarryall or Como.

There was no shelter for the driver of the coach during inclement weather, and winters in the Pikes Peak area often range at 30 degrees below zero. An unknown journalist left this

colorful description of his stagecoach driver.

>   It was interesting to notice this man during his run.
> Whenever he would become cold he would wave his arms
> vigorously and slap his chest. Clad in a great fur overcoat and
> wrapped in buffalo robes from his head to the tip of his toes, he
> was a sight to behold as he peeped out through the opening for his
> eyes. Whenever his hands and fingers would become cold we
> passengers sitting in the rear of the coach would observe him
> winging his lower arms and slapping his hands and fingers upon
> his thighs or body to stimulate the blood circulation. We in the
> rear would often imitate his calisthenic movements but as he
> received squarely in the face the full benefit of the cold wind and
> as we were sheltered by a partition of canvas, we escaped
> considerable of the exposure.
>   ...Gulches and ravines are passed as the stage rolls along
> and steep hills to climb and steep ones to descend are trying times
> for the horses and spicy periods for the driver and the passengers.
> Often there is uncertainty whether the bus [stage] will remain right
> side uppermost and the horses keep from running away. But these
> are but small incidents of the trip that furnish spice and variety.

Each arrival of the stage was a great social occasion in Florissant, and most of the town

crowded around the tired, steaming horses and greeted the dusty, cramped passengers. In the

early days of postal service, each parcel had to be signed for as duly received. Florissant's early

postal ledgers reflect the eager signatures of residents such as Count Pourtales and Adeline

Hornbek and their many neighbors, while Postmaster Frank Castello attested to their identity

with his signature. Neighbors stood around on Piah Street (now Highway 24) waiting for the

A STAGE COACH PREPARES TO LEAVE FLORISSSANT on Piah Street (Highway 24). Passengers usually arrived in Florisssant in time for supper, and then stayed overnight before proceeding to their destination. *(Photo courtesy Colorado Springs Pioneers Museum)*

stage as they swapped bits of gossip and news. Stage Coach drivers were pressed for news from Colorado Springs, and heavy bundles of the *Gazette Telegraph* were burst open and read voraciously.

Daniel Nevitt operated the Florissant House where many of the stage guests stayed overnight. It was probably this business relationship that fostered the friendship between Nevitt and Allen, the stagecoach driver. When young William (Bill) Allen later homesteaded in Florissant, he worked for Dan Nevitt for a while. He later worked for Charles McLaughlin, brother of stage line owner Matthew McLaughlin, who operated a general store with his partner John Horrigan. They had bought the Florissant Mercantile from Frank Castello about 1892.

PIAH, **EXTRAORDINARILY** **HANDSOME TABEGUACHE** **CHIEF,** for whom the main street in Florissant was named. Piah was Chipeta's brother and was a great favorite of Denver society. *(Photo courtesy Denver Public Library)*

Bill Allen then bought and operated the post office and drug store next door.

Bill Allen had an extremely eventful year in 1891. First, a horse fell on him, pinning his leg under a piece of wood lying on the ground. His aunt, who was a doctor, was visiting from California at the time. She recognized the signs of blood poisoning, and urged that Bill be taken to the hospital in Colorado Springs. His father and aunt loaded him in the farm wagon, and started on their way. They arrived at Silas Thompson's ranch in Divide about midnight. Attie and Silas made room for Bill and his family, and Silas sent one of his hired men for the doctor at Manitou.

When the doctor arrived the next morning, he saw that he needed to amputate the injured leg immediately. When this was done, Bill was again loaded in the wagon and taken on down the pass to Manitou. After he had been there a few days, the doctors had to operate a second time, taken a little more of the poisoned flesh and bone. Bill was left with a stub just below the knee.

About five years later, in 1895, Bill Allen rode out to Silas Thompson's ranch to visit Thompson's wife, Atlanta (Long) Thompson. Ironically, "Attie" had just had her leg amputated, and it was Bill Allen's turn to lend her moral support. A doctor had to come up from Colorado Springs to do the surgery. As there was no hospital, her doctor made an operating table out of some rough boards covered with a comforter. Bill commiserated with Attie over the loss of her leg, warning her of using too much morphine for the pain, and saying, "Well, they could cut all my arms and legs off and I would never take it again."

Allen's second major event of the year was of a more pleasant nature—marriage. He and his brother Silas each married one of the Dodge sisters, Dora and Flora, respectively. The girls had come to Florissant with their parents, Emma and Jonathan E. Dodge, Jr., from Missouri. When Bill Allen later bought the Florissant Mercantile (about 1898), his father-in-law, Jonathan Dodge, operated the drug department for him.

By 1889, there were about 150 residents in the Florissant area. Homesteaders, ranchers and other settlers continued to find their amusement in many of the same simple ways as they

SILAS AND ATLANTA (LONG) THOMPSON, circa 1890. Atlanta and Silas led remarkable lives in their effort to make a home in Pikes Peak backcountry. Atlanta had to have a leg amputated without the benefit of painkiller or hospital. She and Silas also suffered the heartbreaking loss of two of their infant daughters.
(Photo courtesy Douglas & Virginia Pearce)

had ten years before. Cattle roundups, berry picking, and the arrival of the stagecoach were still major social events. Barn dances were now so large that they were held either at the new schoolhouse or at one of the sawmills.

Frances Bass writes that there was little social distinction at these affairs. One would probably find the Count and Countess Pourtales swinging to the strains of the Virginia Reel and the quadrille along with Adeline Hornbek, the Allens, Burnhams, McLaughlins, Castellos, Longs, Thompsons, and other families of the area. One of the favorite musicians for these dances was Jesse Cook. He always drove to the dance in a homemade, horse-drawn cart, bringing his faithful dog with him. His price for an evening of his fiddle music was $5 plus a

DORA DODGE ALLEN, circa 1895.

Dora and her twin sister, Flora, married the Allen brothers, William (Bill) and Silas. Dora loved her life in the mountains at Twin Creek Ranch, and lived there until the ranch was finally sold in 1946.

(Photo courtesy Marge & Don Christiansen)

WILLIAM C. ALLEN, circa 1895.

Allen purchased the Florissant Mercantile around 1898, and later acquired Twin Creek Ranch when a Cripple Creek miner defaulted on his grubstake. Like Atlanta (Long) Thompson, he also had to have his leg amputated after a horse fell on it.

(Photo courtesy Marge & Don Christiansen)

piece of cake for his dog. "If his dog didn't get any cake, Jesse didn't play the fiddle."

Entire families attended these dances, bringing everyone from one to ninety-one to eat and dance and socialize. This included eligible young daughters, who served as magnets for the lonely cow punchers who spent most of their lives tending cattle in remote mountain pastures. These young men were chivalrous and held women in high esteem, always treating them with frontier gallantry. They wore the best clothes that they could buy, and took great pride in their appearance. It was not unusual for them to spend a month's wages for a fine pair of custom-made boots. The late historian Granville Stuart wrote a colorful description of the typical cow puncher in the 1927 issue of *The Cascade Courier*.

> Their trappings consisted of a fine saddle, silver mounted bridle, pearl-handled six shooter, latest model cartridge belt with silver buckle, silver spurs, a fancy quirt with silver mountings, a fine riata sometimes made of rawhide, a pair of leather chaps, and a fancy hat band often made from the dressed skin of a diamond-backed rattlesnake. They wore expensive stiff-brimmed light felt hats, with brilliantly colored silk handkerchiefs knotted about their necks, light colored shirts and exquisitely fitted, very high heeled riding boots [with trousers tucked into their boot].

A cowboy's first priority on riding into town for a dance was to see that his horse was properly cared for at the livery stable. He next visited Calas Wilson at his barber shop, for a close shave and a much-needed haircut—and perhaps even a bath. Dances were also the occasion for potluck suppers, but the "waddies" and "buckaroos" were seldom asked to pray over the food. Their pithy and humorous graces were a little too outrageous for most of their hosts.

> "Eat the meat and leave the skin;
> Turn up your plate and let's begin."

Another irreverent grace went something like the following:

> "Yes, we'll come to the table
> As long as we're able
> And eat every damn thing
> That looks sorter stable."

At dawn the next morning, the tired dancers would all pile into their farm wagons to head home, huddled against the cold mountain air under layers of blankets and comforters. The buckaroos would mount their wiry mustangs, and whoop and yell as they bucked their way out of sight.

Crofutt's 1885 *Grip Sack Guide of Colorado* reports that Colorado Springs now boasted over 5,000 residents, and nearby Colorado City another 350. Dr. Bell, a close friend of General William Palmer, had built a fine hotel just north of what later would become Woodland Park. Little London's society delighted in traveling into the mountains to Bell's Manitou Park and Hotel. Atlanta (Long) and Silas Thompson had built a fine ranch at Hayden's Divide, where there were several other ranches in the area although no town as yet.

South of the Thompson's Divide ranch, near a place called Sheep Rock, a group of horse thieves set up operations from about 1876 until 1880. Stealing horses seems to have been a lucrative business around this time, as a second such outfit also set up business on nearby

COWBOY OF THE 1800s. The gypsy lifestyle of the cowboy meant that home was where ever he hung his hat. Consequently, hat, boots and saddle were of prime importance--often costing an entire month's pay. *(Photo courtesy Ute Pass Historical Society)*

Cabin Creek (in what is now Mueller Park). This second group of entrepreneurs was known locally as the White Brothers. These brothers worked from the neighborly confines of two small cabins in what is now called Horsethief Gulch. They were astute enough not to steal from their neighbors, and instead preyed on the hapless citizens of Pueblo and Canon City. "Liberated" horses were stealthily herded to their base of operations, where they were rested and rebranded. They were then taken to the lucrative markets in Denver. The White Brothers made a comfortable living in this manner, and didn't retire until around 1918 when the automobile displaced the horse in popularity.

Canon City also benefited from the increased traffic to the gold fields, and now had a population of about 2,500. A State Penitentiary was built there, and incarcerated about 200 prisoners—more people than lived in the entire Florissant area. Hamilton, on the Tarryall Road, still had about 100 people in the area, and Fairplay had received a second life and now had about 500 residents.

Adeline Hornbek's ranch had greatly increased in value. When she first filed for her homestead, the property was worth $1200. She now had 21 horses, over 100 cows, 3 swine and 50 poultry. She had sown thirty acres in hay and twenty acres in Irish potatoes. By 1885, her ranch was valued at nearly $6,000. Adeline was a success. She had survived a flood, financial ruin, death of one husband and abandonment by another. She, her daughter and her three boys had made a very good life for themselves.

Adeline was not a pretty woman, but she had a commanding presence with dark eyes gazing resolutely from a square, thickset face supported by square, thickset shoulders, and crowned with a coronet of flaming red hair. The story of her life would end happily when she again married at the age of sixty-six.

This time the lucky man was a Prussian emigrant named Frederick Sticksel, and the two traveled extensively in the United States and Europe. Adeline died of paralysis in 1905 at the ripe old age of seventy-two. She was laid to rest in the Four Mile Cemetery just south of the Florissant Fossil Beds.

SODA SPRINGS AND GUARD HOUSE AT CANON CITY circa 1880. In January 1868, the Colorado legislature established a State Penitentiary in Canon City. The first prisoner was incarcerated there in 1871. By 1880, the Penitentiary boasted a larger population (200 Inmates) than all of Pikes Peak backcountry. *(Photo courtesy Ute Pass Historical Society)*

In 1973, the government bought her old homestead to renovate it in time for the 1976 bicentennial celebration. It was incorporated into the boundaries of the Florissant Fossil Beds National Monument. Then in 1981, her homestead was placed on the National Register of Historic Places. This is a fitting tribute to a truly remarkable woman.

CHAPTER VII: CON ARTISTS RAILROAD A MINING HOAX,

AND THE MIDLAND RAILROAD ARRIVES

Coloradans shared a common ailment in the latter half of the 1800s—gold fever. Residents of the state had become inured to Colorado's unlimited amounts of precious metals, simply waiting to be found. A staccato succession of gold and silver finds throughout the state had made a reality of this perception. Hayden's surveys, published in a series of Annual Reports, only validated this assumption, as they glowingly detailed the rich geological resources of the state. Thus, when anyone merely breathed the word "gold," most were only too ready and willing to jump up and head for the Rockies with their bedrolls and miner's picks.

An enterprising scoundrel, S.J. Bradley, concocted a devious scheme to capitalize on this gold fever. History books have labeled it the "Mount Pisgah Hoax," which was an exacerbation of the lie itself—Mount Pisgah was actually about fourteen miles east of Bradley's salted McIntyre Mountain.

Bradley had earlier schooled himself on mining hoaxes in a similar swindle in Leadville. In the fall of 1883, Bradley did some prospecting on the Gribble ranch just north of Canon City, and ten miles southwest of Florissant, near McIntyre Mountain. In the spring of 1884, Bradley returned with a band of eight conspirators from Leadville. Together, they excavated, panned, and constructed placer operations on their respective twenty-acre claims. Bradley and D.G. Miller dug a sizable eighteen-foot trench into Gribble's pasture and labeled it "Teller Placer, 7 April 1884." They then loaded some of the placer's supposed ore samples into a wagon and drove to the nearest assay office, thirty-five miles south in Canon City. Reports from the assay tests were explosive—they ranged from 4 to 107 ounces of gold per ton. Just one wheel barrow full of ore could be worth $80 to $200. Announcements of this tremendous gold discovery were headlined in newspapers all over Colorado. The stampede was on!

Gold seekers swarmed to this new El Dorado, first by the hundreds, then by the thousands. Each man staked out a twenty-acre claim, and soon the pasture for miles around McIntrye Mountain was pockmarked with the diggings of frenzied miners. Bradley sat atop his claim with a loaded shotgun, just in case a claim jumper might take a fancy to his Teller Placer. He and his partners had the "foresight" to draw up maps, diagrams, pamphlets, and stock certificates—ready for sale when the first would-be millionaires arrived.

The Rio Grande Railroad ran special trains from Denver to Pueblo and Canon City; the South Park train carried prospectors to Como and Buena Vista; the road through Ute Pass was reminiscent of the Leadville boom days. The Colorado Springs *Daily Gazette* enthused about the quality of the road through Ute Pass, sniffing that the "Denver papers, in the interests of Canon City, satirically or ironically, but certainly untruthfully, refer to as the 'terrors of the Ute Pass road.'" In an attempt to "show the apparently purchased untruthfulness of the assertions of those newspapers which have characterized the Ute Pass road as a dangerous and the longest route to the scene of the late gold excitement" the *Gazette* published (on 4/25/1884) a detailed

description of the journey up Ute Pass to the gold strike.

By the route we traversed, which is certainly the best one from any railway point into the exploded mining section, the distance is forty-six miles from Colorado Springs, made up as follows:

From Colorado Springs to Summit Park [Woodland Park] Postoffice	16 mi.
Thence to South Park house	3 mi.
Thence to Copeland's ranch house [Coplen's Ranch, Florissant]. . . .	9 mi.
Thence to Four Mile road	4 mi.
Thence to Root's ranch house	2 mi.
Thence to Kittredge's ranch house. .	7 mi.
Thence to alleged gold mines, Appropriately termed "Suckerville" .	5 mi.
Total. . .	46 mi.

We divided the route up thus in order to indicate stopping places, or places which one must branch off from the main travelled road.

At the Summit Park [Woodland Park] postoffice, where is located the old "Junction house," (now closed up temporarily) we left Manitou Park road on our right, and proceeded on the main Leadville or Fairplay road. At the South Park house, kept by Mr. Jas. K. Fical, late of Cheyenne Canon, we found excellent accommodations for man and beast, including clean, warm beds for the former.

At Copeland's [Coplen's Ranch, Florissant] one may find good food and clean beds, and a hearty welcome. On top of the first hill beyond Copeland's [Coplen's], and about three-fourths of a mile from his house, the road branches to the right and left. We took the left-hand road. So also at the Four Mile road, four miles beyond Copeland's [Coplen's], we kept to the left.

At Root's ranch we obtained a nice dinner, with excellent coffee. Just before reaching this point we met Mr. B. Lowe, of the "Times," and Mr. Baird, the mining expert, who gave us the first reliable news of the barrenness of the prospect ahead of us at our journey's end. We reached Colonel Kittredge's early in the afternoon, but as he had been up to the camp and as we could obtain much preliminary and valuable information from him; and as, moreover, we were assured of a generous and acceptable entertainment for ourselves and animals at his hands and under his spacious roof, we concluded to defer our entry into the camp until the following day (Thursday) and remain with him over night.

The main road branches right and left at Kittredge's. We left his house to the left and proceeded by the right-hand road along West Four Mile creek in a direction almost due west [about five miles].

The *Gazette* reported that Bradley's hoax had drawn as many as five thousand men to McIntrye Mountain in just a few short weeks. It didn't take long for some of the more wizened prospectors to sense that there was something very wrong as they dug around in the non-auriferous granite, trachite, loam and sandstone. A number of these men dug a shaft next to Bradley's to test the genuineness of the assays. As suspected, the "Teller" had been salted! The *Gazette* published a report by the Committee Sent to "Suckerville," concluding that "the latter covering assays made at Colorado College of samples of stuff brought from the Alleged mines ... will speak for themselves, and show why this mining boom, the greatest and quickest that Colorado had ever known, was so speedily exploded."

Two of Colorado's greatest gold discoveries were designated as being near Mount Pisgah.

Ironically, the first discovery—the Pisgah Hoax of 1884—was immediately accepted as being authentic. The second discovery, which was the authentic multi-million dollar Cripple Creek bonanza of 1891, was rejected at first as a hoax.

In addition to exposing the Pisgah Hoax, the stories of the *Gazette* also brought to light the problems of declining use of the Ute Pass Wagon Road. The *Gazette* intimated that this lack of use was the result of a clever propaganda campaign waged by the cities of Denver and Canon City. These two cities hoped to cut into the lucrative business of outfitting prospectors on their way to the gold fields. As a result, the merchants of Colorado City and Colorado Springs were feeling the impact.

The true culprits, instead, were the railroads. In 1879, the Denver South Park & Pacific line was laid into South Park all the way to Weston Pass road, and soon reached all the way to Buena Vista. By July, 1880, Palmer's Rio Grande ran to Pueblo and then wound along the Arkansas until it reached all the way to Leadville itself. Morris Cafky writes that as a result, "The Ute Pass wagon road sank back to a placid existence, serving the needs of ranchers in the country west of Pikes Peak and providing an outlet to market for several lumbering firms in the region."

In fact, it was the lumbering activities at Summit Park that ultimately led to the rebirth of the Ute Pass Wagon Road as a parallel path for the Colorado Midland Railroad. About two miles north of Summit (Woodland) Park, an enterprising logger named Homer D. Fisher cast about for a way to make his operation more efficient. His outfit produced telephone and telegraph poles, railroad ties, and mining and bridge timbers for customers in Colorado Springs. In 1881, he sought to cut the costs of hauling these timber products by constructing an eight-mile, narrow gauge railroad from the timber-cutting area down to his sawmill. Fisher leased the locomotive, named "Ouray", from his friend General Palmer for the next eight years. Ironically, it had to be dragged up Ute Pass by mule team in order to reach his logging site.

"Ouray" was a great success in cutting Fisher's costs. It didn't take long before Fisher sought to apply this same solution to the transportation of his finished lumber down Ute Pass to Colorado Springs. Merchants in Colorado City and Colorado Springs often shared their pipe dream of a railroad up Ute Pass and westward into Colorado's gold mining towns. Fisher seized upon this idea as also solving his transportation needs. It was cumbersome and expensive to haul his products down Ute Pass using wagons drawn by oxen and mules. He had already proved to himself the efficiency and economy of railroads with the short "Ouray" line at his lumber camp. Doggedly, Fisher set about making his vision a reality.

Fisher arranged to have a noted railroad engineer, Thomas Wigglesworth of the Denver & Rio Grande, make a preliminary survey through Ute Pass. With this expert opinion supporting his concept, Fisher then went about organizing a railroad company, and in November of 1883, the Articles of Incorporation for the Colorado Midland Railway were filed with the State of Colorado. Inertia then set in as sufficient funding to build the railroad eluded its visionaries. At last, in 1885, their idea sparked the interest of a newcomer to the area, James John Hagerman.

Hagerman had arrived in Colorado Springs the year before, hoping to vanquish the tuberculosis which threatened his life. He had previously amassed a fortune in Milwaukee with his iron smelters. When he arrived in Colorado, his health rapidly improved and he was soon casting about for something to relieve his boredom. His energies quickly vented themselves in the mining industry, as he took possession of Aspen's Mollie Gibson silver mine, and several coal mines near Glenwood Springs. Hagerman was quick to see how the proposed Colorado Midland Railroad (CMRR) would facilitate shipping both his silver ore and his coal to the markets in Colorado Springs and beyond. Haggerman joined the corporation, and was soon applying all of his business acumen in raising the construction funds.

Building a standard gauge railroad through the Colorado Rockies, as the CMRR proposed, was considered a radical idea in 1884. Narrow gauge railroads were better able to navigate the steep mountain passes and narrow winding canyons of the Rockies than were standard gauge. So while almost all of America's trains sang along standard gauge tracks, they hit a virtual "iron curtain" when they reached the base of the Rocky Mountains. The railroad tracks from Denver south to Colorado Springs reflected this conundrum—for they were laid with three rails in order to accommodate both standard and narrow gauge.

At this point, however, cargo destined for points west had to be off-loaded from the standard gauge and then re-loaded onto the narrow gauge—a time consuming and costly undertaking.

Construction contracts were let by the CMRR in April, 1886. Hagerman and his new

Chief Engineer Wigglesworth, or "Wig" as Hagerman called him, began a frenzy of activity in charting the path for their history-making standard gauge. By March, 1887, the CMRR's rails had been spiked down all the way to Florissant, and by June they had reached Buena Vista. Ute Pass had been conquered by the CMRR standard gauge!

On each side of Hayden's Divide, the grades of the track were laid for a 3% climb—a three foot climb for every hundred feet of track. This engineering glitch—standard gauge performance was intended for no more than a 2% grade—insured Florissant's future for the next forty years. Helper engines were needed to assist each train over Hayden's Divide, and Florissant became their home.

Within a year, the CMRR erected an elaborate passenger and freight depot in Florissant (where the Thunderbird Inn now sits), and began construction on a large roundhouse for sheltering the six helper engines to be stationed there. There were also a telegraph office, a bunk house, and a large assemblage of corrals and stock pens. A large wooden water tank, across from the station (where the Fossil Inn now sits), supplied water pumped from Twin Creek with a steam pump. When the first train rolled through Florissant on July 13, 1887, the residents were jubilant, and met its arrival with all the pomp and circumstance the little town could muster.

Construction of the railroad provided a boom for the sawmills up and down the line, as the railbed was built using mostly native pine for the trestles. Atlanta (Long) Thompson and her husband Silas benefited from this demand and also from boarding many of the men working

COLORADO MIDLAND RAILROAD TRAIN PREPARES TO DEPART FLORISSANT, circa 1887.

The handsome station building would be moved to the nearby fossil beds in 1922 where it would serve as a hotel. *(Photo courtesy Marge & Don Christiansen)*

on the tracks near their ranch in Divide. Nevitt's and Coplen's both benefited by increased occupancy at their hotels, as did Gill's, Bean's, and Allen's sawmills. Florissant's population jumped from about 70 in 1885 to well over 150 by 1887, as about twenty-two railroad men and their families moved into town to work for the CMRR.

Florissant's one-room log school house could not accommodate all of the new students. A building fund was begun in 1886, and Frank Castello sold an acre of land to School District Number 13 for $1.00. Coldwell and Spoon received the $884 contract to build the school, and

COLORADO MIDLAND RAILROAD ENGINE #17 and engineer Frank Smith. The Midland's engines were gaily colored, with gun-metal blue smoke stacks mounted on bright green tenders, and backed with a beautiful redwood cabin for the engineer. *(Photo courtesy Carl Quist)*

began construction in the summer of 1887. In October, they were awarded an additional $66 to build two privies, artfully screened with Victorian latticework.

Florissant's little log school was sold to the high bidder for $17. No records have been found on the exact location of this original log school, but it was probably located near the Florissant Cemetery on Upper Twin Rocks Road.

Florissant's merchants were no longer the ruling class in the little community. Veterinarian Dr. H. A. Burton, whose father was an engineer for the Colorado Midland, wrote

CHILDREN ON THEIR 1800s SCHOOL BUS AT BETHEL SCHOOL. This one-room log schoolhouse was probably very similar to the building that Florissant replaced in 1887. Students, (L-R): Dorothy Feizel, Oscar Mascick, Merrill Daw, Cora Mace, Wesley Daw, Alice Haggerty Jeffryes. *(Photo courtesy of Marge & Don Christiansen)*

vividly of the ensuing conflict in Cafky's *Colorado Midland.*

In its heyday, Florissant had several general stores and other business houses. These did a good business catering to the railroad employees and to the ranchers and farmers in that part of the west Pikes Peak country. Naturally, the merchants tried to run the town, and often did so, much to the annoyance of many of the railroaders and ranchers.

The railroaders and the ranchers became aware of the fact that they constituted quite a voting bloc in a town as small as Florissant. There were six locomotive engineers stationed there, nine firemen, two water service men operating the pumphouse on day and night shifts, a couple of men who shoveled coal from gondolas to the locomotives—there was no coal chute—Mr. Banner, the station agent, a night telegraph operator and my father, the road foreman. The farm and ranch population was larger, of course.

Finally, when a school election was approaching, Dad tossed his hat in the ring as a candidate for Teller County School Board. Opposing him was a Florissant merchant. After a vigorous campaign, Dad was elected. There was a great celebration on the railroad when the votes were tallied—whistles blew and bells rang on all the helper engines present in town at the moment the results were known, and cheers floated into the air from the Midland tracks. All was quiet around the "business district" as the merchants were very unhappy.

Florissant continued to grow and prosper, and in 1889 the school board voted unanimously to build an addition on the east side of the white frame building. This time the contract, for $1,310, was awarded to the Allen family—original homesteaders and noted carpenters.

Standardization of school construction had been established in the early 1800s, and Florissant's new school proudly conformed. White, framed, one-room schools within walking distance of the family ranch or farm were duplicated within most townships of the state. These little schools were generally modest, with windows along both sides, and an entrance at one end. Ornamentation consisted of a potbellied stove and a blackboard.

Students sat on wooden benches and committed their lessons to small, square slates. Each student usually carried a small jar of water and a rag with which they cleaned their slate

FLORISSANT'S NEW WHITE FRAME SCHOOL, BUILT 1887. Prosperity brought by the Colorado Midland Railroad enabled residents to replace the one-room log school with this beautiful new building. Note the white rail fence surrounding the school. This was to keep the open-range cattle from harming the children during recess. *(Photo courtesy Denver Public Library)*

in between lessons. Older and more capricious children would dispense with the bottle and rag, substituting a bit of spittle and the sleeve of their shirt.

Florissant's little white school was built with its entryway facing south, toward the Ute Pass Wagon Road and West Twin Creek. This little room was lined with brass coat hooks on one wall and wooden shelves on the opposite wall. These shelves were used by students to store their lunch buckets, made from a half-gallon size lard or syrup pail. Most lunches consisted of a jelly sandwich, or perhaps a fried egg sandwich, placed on thick slices of homemade bread or

SCHOOLS IN THE 1800s WERE USUALLY LOCATED WITHIN A 5-MILE WALK OR RIDE FROM THE HOMESTEAD. Nate Snare would later write, "we kids tried riding to school in the winter on burros, which wasn't so good, so we walked most of the time, two and a half miles each way." *(Photo courtesy Ute Pass Historical Society)*

biscuits. It wasn't unusual to find that the bread had frozen while sitting in the anteroom, and had to be toasted on the top of the pot-bellied stove. These sandwiches were washed down by cold spring water, brought up from the Creek and shared from a common dipper.

With the addition to the school in 1889, Florissant loosened its purse strings for an embellishment—a large bell tower with a Queen Ann-style turret. This school bell was essential to the life of the Florissant community. It not only called the children to school, but also rang

CHIEF SEVERO'S CHILDREN circa 1875. In sharp contrast to their white counterparts, Ute children did not receive formal education until their containment on Reservations which required attendance at boarding schools. Chief Severo worked closely with Chief Buckskin Charlie in helping his people adapt to reservation life. *(Photo courtesy Ute Pass Historical Society)*

in case of any emergency, especially fire. Somewhere around this same time, the school district also added a shack for storing coal out behind the schoolhouse. This shack was later used in the early 1900s as a cook shack when hot meals were served to the children. A teacher's residence was also added in the early 1900s. All of these buildings, including the school, were placed on the National Register of Historic Places in 1991.

Florissant was primarily a ranching community in the 1800s, and so the school year usually commenced in October after the fall roundup. Classes were held for only six months, and the children were sent home at the end of April in order to help with calving and the spring roundup.

As in most rural communities, Florissant's schoolhouse became the focus of all the local activities. In addition to being used for the education of the community's children, Florissant's schoolhouse was also used for weddings, church services, funerals, and as the Polling Place on election day. As one pioneer wrote, "There were many gatherings at the schoolhouse during the years. At Christmas and at the end of the year there were programs, parties, and dinners. The favorite gatherings were dances." Florissant's school was the "heart of the community. People liked to go there and visit friends from up and down the valley."

One of the more unusual "students" at the Florissant school was fondly remembered by Dr. H. A. Burton.

> Dad was an engineer for the Colorado Midland and would have four helper engines pulling the train up the four [three] percent grade to Divide. One day they hauled a load of sheep to Divide and dad returned to Florissant with one of the helper engines. He saw this small lamb beside the track, apparently it was born and fell out of the freight car, so he stopped the engine and brought the lamb back with him to Florissant. Mother bottle-fed this lamb, which got to be a real pet to us kids and would follow us to school. It would sit out on the school steps and follow us around during recess, then tag us home. On the hill back of our home, (the first house on the right side as you now come into Florissant), there was nothing but a prairie dog village - thousands of these prairie dogs. The government had a drive to get rid of them, having poison grain put out to kill them. The sacks of poison were down by the depot and some of it spilled out

on the ground, Our lamb, who walked all over Florissant, ate some of the poison and died. My brother brought her home in a wheelbarrow and we had a regular funeral out in our back yard for that lamb we all loved; mother even read some verse from the bible.

Frank Castello's Mercantile encountered its first full-fledged competitor in 1890. Partners J.S. Lentz and J.E. Handbury began operation of the Handbury & Lentz General Store. They hired William (Bill) Spell as their head bookkeeper; for the store, for their two sawmills, and for their lumber yard. Spell had recently moved from Hugoton, Kansas, in order to escape a bloody feud with the rival town of Woodsdale over which town should become the county seat. He had followed several of his other Kansas friends to the Florissant area, notably George Carr and Alec King.

In the summer of 1890, the rivalry between the two general stores took on a more sinister dimension. Three bandits attempted to hold up Castello's post office and store shortly after the monthly payday. Castello had been warned, probably by George Carr, and was prepared. He had his watchman and several others waiting to ambush the would-be bandits. Shots were fired and one of the robbers was injured. However, they all were able to mount their horses and race into the timbered hills.

Early the next morning, Florissant's Marshal Ed Bell deputized a posse and set off after the robbers. (One of the posse members was none other than the lackadaisical cowboy Bob Womack.) They followed the trail all that day and through the night. Early on the second morning they surprised the outlaws, camped in a small valley near Sedalia, casually preparing their breakfast. Bell gave no chance for surrender, but instead opened fire on the three men. One of the men, a young man of about twenty, was killed instantly. His two companions dashed for the woods, and eluded the posse. Marshall Bell gathered their horses, throwing the body of the young man across one, and brought them back to Florissant.

Feelings ran high in Florissant, and most of the townspeople pressed simply to bury the young man in a hole in the ground. Bill Spell argued that the young man deserved a coffin and a decent burial, and prevailed upon the citizens. When the young man was identified, and his family came to bury him, it was learned that he came from a very good family of modest wealth.

Spell's sons were able to identify the horses of the other two outlaws as belonging to former neighbors from Kansas. Castello questioned Spell's previous acquaintance with the two holdup men, Noble and Robinson, and his seemingly unwarranted interest in the proper burial of the young outlaw. Even though it was later found that it was Alec King who had masterminded the attempted robbery, Castello still viewed Spell with a jaundiced eye. As a result of this incident, distrust and friction smoldered between the rival stores of Castello and Handbury & Lentz (Spell's employers) for years afterward.

Ranching remained the primary source of Florissant's economy even after the advent of the Colorado Midland Railroad. Actually, the railroad provided a boost to the ranching community. It was now possible for area ranchers to herd their cattle into nearby Florissant to

ROUNDUP WEST OF LAKE GEORGE, AUGUST 1895. Virtually all of Pikes Peak backcountry was open range, and fences were nonexistent. Note the pole corrals being used to collect the cattle. *(Photo courtesy Ute Pass Historical Society)*

the CMRR stockyards. There they awaited one of the freight trains which then hauled them to the markets in Colorado Springs or to the gold camps in the central mountains. This saved the ranchers the trouble and expense of driving their cattle to market over long, dusty trails. It also allowed the cattle to be sold at a much higher weight, for the long foot-trek to market inevitably caused a material loss of valuable pounds on each cow.

Most of the country and Pikes Peak's western slope was still open range available to everyone. Area ranchers simply branded their stock, and then turned them out onto the lush mountain pastures to graze where they might. Early each spring, the ranchers would get

181

together and designate representatives or "reps" for the roundup, designate the roundup area on certain creeks, and set a roundup date.

At the designated time and place, the reps and cowboys from the different outfits gathered. A roundup boss was elected, and then they all began to comb the hills and valleys and to bunch the cattle they collected into pole corrals or box canyons. Pole corrals were portable and were easily constructed, as they required only a hatchet to chop down the tall, slender aspen or pine trees. These trees were then laid atop one another, parallel to the ground in a zig-zag pattern.

Once the cattle were gathered into the corrals, the cows and their calves were sorted and the calf was given the same brand as his mother. Bawling calves and their bellowing mothers filled the pure mountain air with a cacophony of fear-filled voices. Acrid smoke from the branding fire and calves' singed hide mingled with the sickly smell of blood from the de-horning saw and the castration knife.

Anne Hawkins wrote of watching her older brother at spring roundup one year in the 1927 (?) *Independent*.

> ...I remember hearing my cowpuncher brother describe a very "busy" time he had with an irate cow critter. They were branding inside a pole corral and he was just ready to put the iron on the calf when the old cow charged him. He didn't have time to do a thing but roll over on his back and begin kicking dust in that cow's eyes and while she was shaking it out and wiping her eyes, brother made the top of the fence. "Fly for the fence, boys. She's on the prod." was a familiar slogan in those days—as familiar as "Railroad crossing, look out for the cars" is in these days, and

much more effective. I have vivid memories of the burning hair when the hot iron was put on the poor little bawling calf calling for his ma-ma, and I presume that is one reason I am not more partial to a marcel. I am sure it must have been every little calf's ambition to be a maverick.

Mavericks were orphaned calves whose ownership was doubtful. It was up to the Roundup Boss to come up with an equitable method of allocating these unbranded cattle. On at least one occasion, ownership was determined during the nightly rounds of poker among the cowboys. One old timer recalled such a poker game where "They played for unbranded cattle, yearlings at 50 cents a head and the top price for any class was five dollars a head."

Once the spring calf crop had been branded, castrated, dehorned, and ears cropped, the animals were turned loose again. They then spent the intervening summer months grazing on the rich mountain grasses. In the fall, the entire roundup process was repeated. This time, however, the herd was culled of the calves, any non-producing cows, and any other animal deemed ready for market. These beef were handled with great care, as each pound of their flesh meant more profit at the market. Once the cattle were gathered, they were carefully herded to the nearest railroad siding with its attendant corrals. When these cattle were loaded on the Colorado Midland, their stock trains were given the right-of-way. Passenger trains would be sidetracked in order to let the stock trains through with their precious cargo.

Ranching on the west slope of Pikes Peak was not always easy. Sometimes the winters were extremely harsh, as they were the year that George Frost lost his entire herd when their flanks froze. In a cold wind or blizzard, cattle will generally stand with their backsides to the

CATTLE ROUNDUP AND BRANDING circa 1895. Ranchers in Pikes Peak backcountry helped one another gather, sort and brand their cattle in the spring after the calves were born. *(Photo courtesy Ute Pass Historical Society)*

gale. It was probably for this reason that only their flanks froze. In that tragic winter of 1886-1887, nearly half of all Colorado's open-range stock perished in the blizzards and deep snow.

By far, the advent of barbed wire onto the open range had the most dramatic impact on ranching. Barbed wire, consisting of two wires twisted together with barbs twisted into the wire in varying designs, was first invented around the 1860s. Between 1868 and 1873, there were a total of 11 patents filed with different barbed wire designs. Joseph Glidden became the most famous manufacturer of these thorny fences after he began production in the mid-1870s. Ranchers began to use the stuff to keep their cattle from drifting all over the open ranges.

Unfortunately, however, it was very often instrumental in the deaths of cattle when they were unable to seek shelter from blizzards and predators.

Fred Howarth, an English immigrant who arrived in Florissant about 1889, recalled the days before barbed wire. "You could get on a horse and ride all day in most any direction without having to open gates. The only fences were along Halthusen Lane south of Florissant [now part of the Fossil Beds], the Burnham Lane west of Florissant [along the eastern edge of Twin Creek Ranch], and the Silas Thompson Lane west of Divide." Most of these homesteaders found the barbed wire invaluable in protecting their tracts of cultivated land from the invasion of open-range cattle. Even the ranchers found that they needed to protect their hay fields in order to harvest enough of a crop to prevent another winterkill such as that of 1886-1887.

Cattlemen also forced the railroad to fence its right of way. They effectively lobbied for laws that made the railroads liable for cattle struck by their trains. Fencing these rights of way was cheaper than paying ranchers for cattle stricken by the trains.

The Pikes Peak cattle industry went into a slump in the early 1890s as a result of several severe winters, the encroachment of the railroad, and the increased presence of barbed-wire fences. It was this volatile environment that awaited the first sheep introduced to the area. Sheep naturally found the rich mountain grasses as nourishing and tasty as the range cattle did. But cattlemen generally shared a pathological hatred of sheep growers, contending that sheep, unlike cattle, cropped the grass too closely and killed off valuable pasture lands.

PANORAMIC VIEW OF FLORISSANT circa 1888. A CMRR engine (center) dramatically belches smoke. The new Florissant school is visible beyond the hill on the top right; stockyards are just visible behind the water tower; and engineer Duffy Malone's two-story house marks the left edge of the photo. *(Photo courtesy Colorado Springs Pioneers Museum)*

Most notable of the sheep ranchers was 54-year-old Herman Halthusen. Halthusen first filed on his homestead claim near the present-day Florissant Fossil Beds Visitor's Center in February 1888. (His red barn still sits opposite the gate to the visitor center.) He already had sheep ranches in Colorado Springs and in Leadville.

Halthusen flooded the remaining open range of Florissant and Four Mile Valleys with over 9,000 head of sheep! Understandably, the cattle ranchers were outraged. At most, these

186

same grasslands were capable of supporting only about 1,000 head of cattle. Furthermore, cattle growers were still struggling from the earlier depredations to their herds. Racial overtones were added to the conflict when Halthusen hired Mexican herders for his sheep. The *Denver Times* reported the conflict on October 31, 1900.

> Three days ago the first outbreak occurred, when settlers tore down the herders' tents and posted a notice on a post giving the Mexicans ten days to withdraw from the district under pain of severe punishment. Halthusen was away at the time. He returned to his herd yesterday and was shown the notice. He said nothing, but one of the herders remarked: "We'll be ready for anything that comes." A week of the ten days' grace has passed. Within three more days it is probable there will be a fight or Halthusen's sheep will be withdrawn from the open range.

The situation seems to have smoldered for a while, and then erupted in a second conflict. A follow-up story by the *Denver Times* on December 18, 1900, sheds further light on the situation.

> The sheep and cattle war at Florissant after slumbering for about six or eight weeks seems likely to break forth again. Last Thursday night two lots of dynamite were exploded near Halthusen's house, one blowing the fence around the house into the road, the other wrecking the corral fence where there were 3000 fat sheep, but doing no other damages. The next morning fifteen sticks of powder were discovered in a gunny sack right among the sheep. It is supposed the sheep had cut the fuse by trampling on it. Examination showed the tracks of two men from the corral to where their horses had been tied. Both men had work overshoes.

Halthusen no doubt drew the further ire of area residents by flaunting his material well being. At one time, he was considered a millionaire. In addition to his lovely home and barns, he turned an excellent profit from his sheep growing. One invoice from a Denver hide dealer discloses that in 1895 alone, Halthusen received over $3,000 for his wool. This was at a time when the average annual income for most families in the Florissant area was just $300.

Sally Halthusen, Herman's daughter, further blighted the family name as she searched for a wealthy husband among the new millionaires in Cripple Creek. Marshall Sprague describes Sally in his posthumous book, *The King of Cripple Creek.*

> ...Charlie [MacNeill] was accompanied by a spectacular, big-bosomed, big-hipped girl almost 6 feet tall, named Sally Halthusen, a daughter of a ... sheep-and-grain man. Sally had the outside structure of a Gibson girl. But inside she was packed with fierce desire instead of sweet gentility. She was said to have collected $10,000 from a Denver father to remove her outside structure from the vicinity of his son. Sally liked men as big and husky as herself and she always had a lot of big fellows around. But what she liked most was horses. She could mount the wildest bronc in Colorado and tame him. One of Cripple's finest sights was Sally astride her white thoroughbred moving along Bennett Avenue. Sally, like Georgia Hayden, was on the prowl for a rich man. But, whereas Georgia wanted luxury and social position, Sally just wanted to get going on a horse farm.

In the midst of Florissant's range wars, its lush meadows of wild flowers continued to bloom. Fragile, blue wild iris contrasted with the deeper blues of flax and columbine. Sparks

HALTHUSEN RANCH circa 1895. Sheep rancher Herman Halthusen moved into the Florissant Valley about 1895. He spawned a local version of the range wars when he flooded the area with over 9000 sheep. His barn can still be seen opposite the entrance to the Florissant Fossil Beds National Monument. *(Photo courtesy Florissant Fossil Beds National Monument)*

of bright red-orange Indian paintbrush danced in the mountain breezes against a backdrop of deep blue-purple Pikes Peak penstemon. Lush meadows of pastel-hued loco weed added to the ethereal beauty of these high mountain valleys. It wasn't long before the new Colorado Midland Railroad came up with a way to capitalize on the area's beauty.

Morris Cafky included several interviews about the "Wildflower Express" in his book *Colorado Midland*. Jack Hickman, an engineer on the CMRR, wrote of his experience on these

COLORADO MIDLAND RAILROAD'S WILDFLOWER EXCURSION TRAIN. These immensely popular tourist trains began running in the 1890s, and soon became a Colorado institution. This scenic one-day round trip departed Colorado Springs at 8:45 a.m., turned around at the west end of ElevenMile Canyon, stopped in the Florissant Valley for flower and fossil gathering, and finally returned to the Springs around 5:00 p.m. *(Photo courtesy Pikes Peak Library District)*

excursion trains.

The Colorado Midland, like other railroads of its era, handled a great deal of summertime excursion business. The most famous, of course, were the Wildflower Excursions which ran from Colorado Springs to Spinney and return[ed]. They were very well patronized and there are many old-timers who, to this day, still remember them with pleasure.

Around the turn of the century, the Midland operated still

another summer excursion train, this one between Colorado Springs and Leadville. This train would leave Colorado Springs at 8 A.M., lay over at Leadville for 1 1/2 hours, and return to Colorado Springs at 8 P.M. It was always a three-car train, as I recall. The first car was a combo with a lunch counter in the baggage section—an arrangement later adopted on the Wildflower trains—a coach and a chair car.

W.A. Coffin, whose father was a crew member on the CMRR, also shared his memories of these colorful expeditions.

Dad was often a crew member on the famous Wildflower Excursion trains which rolled daily, each summer, between Colorado Springs and Spinney at the eastern edge of South Park. Those were gala trains. The crew generally took responsibility for choosing stops to pick wild flowers, and looked for spots where flowers were plentiful and in non-hazardous locations. Flower stops were made in the west-bound direction. After stopping for passengers to picnic, usually at Spinney, we turned the entire train on the wye for the trip back to Colorado Springs. Near Florissant there were some fossil beds, and a stop was made here to allow passengers to search for fossils.

The official train photographer was Lloyd Shaw, who later became famous for his Cheyenne Mountain High School dancers. Lloyd would take pictures of people gathered around, and all over the engine, or grouped at the rear of the train.

Dr. H.A. Burton, whose father was a Midland engineer, also told Cafky of his memories of these famous excursion trains.

The Midland's famous Wildflower Excursions proved to be a source of summertime spending money for the children of

DIGGING FOR FOSSILS ON THE EAST EDGE OF FLORISSANT. These tourists on the Wildflower Express have opted to disembark and dig for the treasured fossils themselves. Those who preferred not to dirty their hands instead hired local children to find their fossils. *(Photo courtesy Colorado Historical Society)*

Florissant. We boys looked forward eagerly to the summer tourist season and the daily operation of the flower train.

Near Florissant, and just a short distance from the Midland right-of-way was a large fossil bed. It was the practice of the railroad to stop the excursion train there, and let the passengers who desired to do so hunt for fossils. We kids were always present when the train stopped, and would sell fossils to those tourists who were too lazy to find their own, or who were unable to locate any.

We also sold crystals and attractive stones. These were obtained in occasional hikes to Crystal Peak, north of Florissant.

Another Florissant resident, Jessie Juanita Patten Barr, shared her early memories of the Wildflower Excursion trains.

> During the summer, the Midland Railroad ran a special every week through August. It was known as the flower excursion, with four open cars and always loaded with people. My two brothers and I sold wild columbines at fifty cents a dozen to these tourists. We would get on the train at Florissant, catch a ride up to the fossil beds, and dig fossils to sell. Some brought two dollars. Everyone was interested in them. When the train went on its merry way back to Colorado Springs, we would start our five mile walk home and do our chores after we got there.

Florissant's prosperity gained momentum during these early years after the Midland Railroad arrived. Other small towns along the Ute Pass Wagon Road also sprang to life with the advent of the railroad. Developers were quick to realize the potential of townsites located along the railway, and made haste to ensure their profits.

At the mouth of Ute Pass, the Cascade Town Company was incorporated in 1886. D.N. Heizer, the Mayor of Colorado Springs, became president of the Cascade Town Company, which listed over 100 residents as members. Within the year, the town was surveyed and platted. A few years later, a lake was built and stocked with trout. By 1889, the stately Ramona Hotel was completed and towered over the town for thirty-five years with her elegant Victorian turrets.

Cascade's charm captured the hearts of two 1895 honeymooners, Thomas and Mary Cusack. Cusack was a poor Irish immigrant who made himself a millionaire when he created

BUILT IN 1888, THE ELEGANT HOTEL RAMONA DOMINATES THIS VIEW OF CASCADE.

Cascade Mountain etches the sky above the Ramona, and tracing of the pikes Peak Highway can be seen on Mt. Heizer to the right. *(Photo courtesy Ute Pass Historical Society)*

the outdoor advertising business. He became known as the Billboard King, but ironically prized Cascade for its pristine beauty. Cusack began systematically to purchase property in the town, and in 1920 he purchased the Cascade Town & Improvement Company. In 1923, Cusack built the baronial Marigreen Pines mansion for his beloved Mary. He also purchased a sizeable ranch just south of Florissant, which is now part of the Florissant Fossil Beds National Monument.

Just a few miles up Ute Pass from Cascade, the fertile mountain valley called Ute Pass Park provided the embryo for another small mountain town—Chipita Park. Most of the valley

MARIGREEN PINES, THOMAS CUSACK'S BARONIAL SUMMER HOME IN CASCADE. In 1978, the Cusack family donated the property to the Congregation of the Holy Cross, and the building now serves as the organization's Novitiate. *(Photo courtesy Ute Pass Historical Society)*

had been the property of General Palmer's friend William Blackmore. After his tragic suicide, however, the land was sold to several ranchers and farmers. With the advent of the Colorado Midland Railroad, developers saw the area as having more potential as a town than as fodder for cows. In 1890, the Ute Pass Land and Water Company was incorporated with an eye to transforming the verdant pastures into a lucrative resort. The elegant Ute Hotel opened in the fall of 1890, overlooking the new Midland depot and the five-acre Chipita Lake.

Several more miles up Ute Pass, in 1881, former teamster George Howard paid $600 for

THE COLORADO MIDLAND MAKES A BRIEF STOP IN GREEN MOUNTAIN FALLS circa 1897.

George Howard's cattle pasture was gracefully transformed into this charming scene once the Colorado Midland's tracks were laid through its meadows. *(Photo courtesy Ute Pass Historical Society)*

some promising ranch land that would later become Green Mountain Falls. This transition came about through the efforts of an English real estate developer named W.J. Foster, who gained title to Howard's ranch in 1887. He envisioned a high-class summer resort town. And so Green Mountain Falls Town and Improvement Co. was incorporated in 1887. By the summer of 1888, there were an estimated 500 people living in tents at the new town site.

The small town was further enhanced in 1888 when its lake was excavated. This required the combined efforts of over twenty teams of horses pulling plows. A small island was left in the center of the lake, and it soon sported a charming Victorian gazebo. Green Mountain Falls, the town, was formally incorporated in July, 1890.

As the Midland Railroad wound its way up the Ute Pass, it continued to spawn new towns every few miles. Crystola, the next town up the line, also began as a ranching community, called Trout Park, when several ranching families moved into the area in 1870. They received only threats and harassment from earlier squatters, however, until they proved their resilience. One of these tenacious ranchers was George Sharrock who named his place Junction House.

Henry Clay Childs, Speaker of the U.S. House of Representatives, moved to Trout Park in the late 1870s. Childs and his wife were spiritualists, and entertained a number of psychics and mediums at their small ranch. Childs and other spiritualists organized the Brotherhood Gold Mining and Milling Company in 1897. This unique company proposed to save aspiring miners from the drudgery of locating a mine by utilizing psychic powers instead. Their brochure boasted that "...the prospector is saved the trouble of locating a mine by an accommodating wizard who, instead of locating the future bonanza for himself will locate it for anybody who will put up a sufficiency of cash in advance."

Crystola, the town, germinated from this psychic quest for gold. In 1899, the Company was renamed the Crystola Brotherhood Town, Mine and Milling Company. Still undaunted, the company built a gold processing mill in Crystola Canyon. Nearby, a large stone building was designated as the site for storing the yet un-found gold. Gold never was found, so the widowed

Childs drowned his hopes in the amber fluid of Duffy's Malt Whiskey. When he died, he left his 2000-acre estate to be used as a school for spiritualism. All that is left of his dream is the Crystola Inn, which once served as the town's grocery.

Woodland Park emerged as a fully incorporated town on January 21, 1891. Unlike Crystola, the roots of the new little town were based on something a little more solid than a spiritualist's advice. Daniel Steffa, an area rancher, saw the potential for a tidy profit with the advent of the Colorado Midland Railroad in 1887. He quickly worked to have his pasture land along the railway platted and named his proposed town "Manitou Park." The Colorado Midland Railroad responded by naming its station there "Manitou Park Station." Legitimacy was fully granted, however, when the United States Postal Service opened its Manitou Park Post Office in March of 1888.

Although the area was previously known to travelers along the Ute Pass Wagon Road as Summit Park, Steffa's new name held fast until the town incorporated in 1891. Steffa, no doubt, wished to capitalize on the popularity of Dr. Bell's elegant resort with the same name, located just a few miles north. Water in the west has always been more precious than gold, and Manitou Park was not immune to its importance. The Woodland Park Town Improvement Company was organized in 1890 in order to provide water for the area, and a pipeline and reservoir were built. When the town incorporated in 1891, the name was officially changed to Woodland Park.

In addition to obtaining a water system, it seems that the 122 residents were also greatly

WOODLAND PARK, circa 1887. Main street, or Midland Avenue (Now Highway 24), was still busy even then. The charming building in the upper left corner was the Woodland Hotel. Note the newly laid tracks of the Colorado Midland Railroad in the center of the photo. *(Photo courtesy Ute Pass Historical Society)*

concerned about the character of their community. Their first order of business after incorporation was to pass a morals and decency ordinance three months later. One can only wonder at what event prompted this ordinance to assess a $100 fine for nude or lewd dress on the streets. Bawdy houses and gambling were banned within the town's limits. Drunks were to be both fined and sent to jail. And anyone who beat an animal was to be assessed a $50 fine.

With its moral environment now firmly secured, Woodland Park began to plot a course of steady growth. Noted Colorado historian Frank Hall described the new little town as it

199

appeared in 1891 in his *History of Colorado*.

> Woodland Park is situated on a high broad plateau, 8,484 feet above sea level, and has a protected and sheltered situation. It affords a fine view of Pike's Peak, and near by are Iron and Sulphur Springs, almost hidden by native shrubbery and wild flowers. During the past year a hotel and several cottages and stores have been erected as well as a church and school. Here is also a good-sized lake.

Beyond Woodland Park, the frequency of new towns began to wane. Seven miles west of Woodland, on the Ute Pass Wagon Road—and now along the Midland's railbed—lay a small ranching community called Hayden's Divide. South of the settlement a plateau had provided a temporary camp for F.V. Hayden's survey team in 1873. Ute Pass also reached its summit at Hayden's Divide, with an elevation of 9,198 feet. Ranchers had always referred to the area as a "divide," for its elevation sorted the rains and melting snows into creeks that flowed east into Fountain Creek and ultimately to the Arkansas River, or west into Twin Creek and ultimately into the South Platte River.

Hayden's Divide was primarily a ranching community. Atlanta (Long) Thompson and her husband, Silas, were among the first area ranchers to profit from the advent of the Colorado Midland Railroad. Silas opened a sawmill and provided the Midland with railroad ties and telegraph poles. Atlanta converted their ranch house into a boarding house, providing food and beds for the railroad workers.

DIVIDE, circa 1887. Silas Thompson and other area ranchers diversified their operations to profit from supplying the Colorado Midland Railroad with railroad ties and telegraph poles. The Little Chapel on the Hill is on the upper left. Just below it and to the right is the "Hello Hotel." *(Photo courtesy Mel McFarland)*

Five miles west of Florissant an astute ex-Bostonian, George Washington Frost, also saw a way to make money from the Colorado Midland Railroad. Frost made a small fortune on the sale of his Boston box factory and bought Toll Witcher's ranch south of Florissant around 1886. As recounted in the previous chapter, Frost lost most of his cattle in the blizzard of 1886-87, however.

In an irony befitting a true westerner, Frost saw a way to make "lemonade from his lemon." The same raw cold that cost him his cattle herd could also make him rich. He saw the

LAKE GEORGE, circa 1915. Entrepreneur, and former cattle rancher, George Frost built this lovely home in Lake George in the late 1890s. Unfortunately, it later burned to the ground. (L-R) Land developer O.W. Battles, Tojuy Sandholm with her dog, and "Majors." *(Photo courtesy Midge Harbour)*

Midland as the means to effecting this turnaround and recouping his losses. He prevailed upon his former business associates back East to buy $95,000 worth of stock in his proposed dam on the South Platte River. Frost waited for his newly built lake to freeze, and then began business in earnest. He constructed several large ice storage houses, and then proceeded to sell his "liquid assets" to the Midland for use in their refrigerated box cars. Frost's ice was instrumental in ensuring the safe shipment of fruits and vegetables from the western slope all across Colorado. Perhaps even more importantly, his ice also cooled the beer that quenched the thirst of Colorado's miners.

D.A. Cuthbert related his memories of these shipments in Morris Cafky's *Colorado Midland*.

> In late August and early September of each year, the Grand Valley fruit crop—peaches, principally, although some apples also moved in the Colorado Midland's day—was shipped to Midwestern and eastern markets, as well as to large Colorado communities. Both the C.M. [Colorado Midland] and the D.&R.G. [Denver & Rio Grande] were kept busy moving in empty reefers [refrigerated cars], and hauling the fruit out in solid trainloads of perishables...The fruit blocks were really "given the road" on the Midland, and often came close to making passenger train time. Because of the nature of the perishable freight, refrigerator loads were light as compared with loads handled in freight cars of equal capacity...
>
> Speaking of icing cars, the Midland had an ice cutting operation at Lake George, including a large ice house. Ice trains operated each winter, making round trips between Colorado City and Lake George. Some of the ice was stored at the C.M. ice house at Colorado City for reefer cooling the following summer; the rest was sold to the Santa Fe for the same purpose.

Frost's lake was first called Lidderdale Reservoir, but later came to be called George's Lake. When the community merited its own post office in April, 1891, it was named Lake George. Though Frost's business prospered, his little town did not keep pace. It soon boasted several saloons, a small CMRR depot, blacksmith shop, school and general store, but remained unincorporated.

This new growth up and down the path of the Midland Railroad was bound to bring trouble as well as prosperity. Claude Harris, a fireman for Midland Railroad, left an account

of one of the more interesting troubles that beset the Railroad. This story is vividly recounted

in Morris Cafky's *Colorado Midland*.

One evening in 1910, engineer "Four-Spot" Frank Stewart and fireman Paul Bochman were called to handle Train 3 from Colorado Springs to Leadville. No. 3 was the night passenger run, usually consisting of a baggage car, open platform coach, open platform chair car, a Leadville sleeper and a Denver to Grand Junction sleeper. Frank and Paul's engine was one of the passenger 4-6-0's with 60-inch drivers.

Between Divide and Florissant, where westbound trains descended a 3% grade, it was the custom for the fireman to clean his fire into the ash pan. Then, the ash pan would be emptied during the stop at Florissant. Paul Bochman began this chore just after No. 3 departed from Divide. He happened to look up and noticed that Frank Stewart was looking back intently at the tender. Frank motioned with his thumb at Paul, and the fireman turned around to see a man coming over the coal gate with a rifle.

The intruder forced Frank to stop the train near Pisgah siding, then ordered both enginemen off the locomotive. In climbing down, Frank slipped and fell. He scrambled to his feet unhurt; unknown to the bandit, he now clutched a large stone in his hand.

The two enginemen were marched back to the baggage car by the thug, who then ordered the fireman to pound on the door and arouse the Wells Fargo express messenger. Instead of obeying, Paul ducked under the car and scrambled to the other side of the train; he intended to run back to the coaches and give the alarm. The bandit leaned over and fired under the car at Paul, wounding him. Just as he fired, Frank Stewart brought his stone down on the bandit's head with such force that the man was killed instantly. A moment later, another shot could be heard down Twin Creek Canon [Florissant Canyon]. This second shot led authorities and railroaders to believe that more than one person was involved in the robbery attempt. It seems likely that the dead bandit had ordered the train stopped in the wrong place.

Paul was carried back and placed in a Pullman berth, and the bandit's corpse was placed in the baggage car. At Florissant, a helper engine station, services of another fireman were secured and No. 3 went on to Leadville. Paul Bochman was hospitalized there, recovered from his wound, and was soon back at work. Frank Stewart was presented with a gold watch by the Colorado Midland Railway; details of the incident were engraved thereon. Frank died many years ago, but his descendants still possess the watch.

There is a second, slightly different, variation on this story as recounted by Chester Allen

in an unpublished letter to his niece, Marge Christiansen.

Yes, there was a train hold up and it was described pretty good only the names were wrong. Sam Millward was the engineer who knocked the guy out with a rock then he got the guys gun and killed him with it. I was just a curious kid at the time and was there when they brought the holdup to town and watched the Sheriff probe the bullett [sic] hole, a picture that always stayed with me, he was shot between the right cheek bone and nose just below the eye.

Millwards were our neighbors lived in Uncle Silas [Allen] house across the road at the time and he was allowed to keep the gun and he displayed it a lot of times, was a 38 Colt automatic. Posses rode the hills for a week but came up empty, so 2 got away.

Fortunately, this attempted robbery seems to be the extent of depredations along the new

railroad. Florissant town folk watched the frenzy of growth up and down the old Ute Pass

Wagon Road as the Midland Railroad spread its promise of wealth. Finally, the community jumped on the band wagon and its 242 residents petitioned for incorporation. Their petition was granted, and Florissant celebrated as a fully incorporated town on the 7th of July, 1891.

CHAPTER VIII: "YELLOW" FEVER RAGES DOWN
THE SLOPES OF PIKES PEAK

Who can say why a man would dedicate his life to the search for tiny scraps of yellow metal buried in the earth's bosom. Hardship, back-breaking labor, cold, starvation—these were the intimate friends of Colorado's gold seekers. Robert Service, the premiere poet of America's westward expansion, perhaps touched at the heart of the matter when he wrote the following lines:

> There's gold, and it's haunting and haunting;
>   It's luring me on as of old;
> Yet it isn't the gold that I'm wanting
>   So much as just finding the gold.
> It's the great, big, broad land 'way up yonder,
>   It's the forests where silence has lease;
> It's the beauty that thrills me with wonder,
>   It's the stillness that fills me with peace.

Colorado's "Yellow" Fever epidemic continued from 1858 well into the 1900s, as gold-crazed men swarmed over the Rockies. This sickness of the heart forced the Utes from their ancient and sacred hunting grounds in the Shining Mountains. These hunting grounds carried a heavy price tag, however. They cost the integrity of a fledgling nation, as treaty after treaty was broken when fevered citizens demanded yet more land.

Until 1890, Florissant had been only on the periphery of this frenzy. Soon, however, a grizzled old prospector set in motion the events that forever changed the Pikes Peak Region, the state of Colorado, and the fortunes of the United States.

Marion C. Lankford was an unlikely catalyst for the Cripple Creek boom. Lankford was a veteran of the Civil War in which he had served under General Robert E. Lee. He fled the horrors of the war and its aftermath, building a cabin on the slope of Jones Mountain, near Mount Princeton. A great black mustache ranged across his sunburnt face. Unkempt, ragged clothing on his tall, lanky frame proclaimed the hours he spent swinging a pick at the granite face of the mountain. When the winter snows became too deep, he loaded his few possessions on his burro and sought the comfort of his friends in Florissant—the Spell's.

Snowflakes swirled around the Spell's two-story home, as Lankford and his friend, Bob Womack, traded dreams before the fire in the winter of 1889. Womack boasted of some promising "float"—light weight rock that indicates gold—that he had found while working on the Broken Box Ranch near Mount Pisgah. He was inclined to imbibe a little too freely, but he and Lankford were firmly bound to one another by their passion for gold. Lankford shared his knowledge of prospecting with the younger Womack, and offered suggestions and encouragement. Late the following year, 1890, as the aspens teasingly flaunted their golden leaves, Lankford's protege hit pay dirt when he re-examined an earlier claim.

Womack renamed his earlier, 1886 Grand View Claim, calling it the El Paso instead.

When the ore samples were later assayed by Professor Henry Lamb of Colorado College, they revealed an amazing value of $250 a ton! "Crazy Bob" had at last found his gold mine. He had been infected with the "yellow" fever seventeen years before, when Hayden's survey geologist had predicted that Cripple Creek's volcanic crater most likely held gold. Womack was, at best, a desultory cowboy, using his time on the range to pick at Cripple's crater under the pretext of searching for strays.

George Harker, Adeline Hornbek's son, also worked his family's cattle in the Cripple Creek area. Harker later told C.S. Dudley of the *Gazette Telegraph* that he and other stockmen would tell Womack that "he was wasting his time; that nothing would come of it for him." Harker said that Womack would invariably answer, "Just wait. You'll see. I'll find gold. Just wait and see."

In spite of the high assay value of Womack's ore, he had difficulty in raising the fifteen to twenty thousand dollars required to remove the ore from his mine. Potential investors in Colorado Springs were still smarting from the Pisgah Hoax, and weren't about to be suckered again. However, Womack's friend and mentor, Marion Lankford, did believe in the erstwhile cowboy.

Late in February of 1891, Lankford convinced his friends from Florissant—William Spell, the Justice of the Peace, and Handbury and Lentz, who owned the general store—to grubstake and outfit him. This group included George Carr, foreman of the Broken Box Ranch, as their fourth partner. As soon as the February weather permitted, Lankford explored the area around the Carr ranch. Just as Womack had reported, Lankford soon found gold-bearing ore in a gulch about a mile and a half from the ranch house. When he returned to Florissant with ore samples, the partners decided that Spell should return with him to Cripple Creek to stake their claims.

Spell and Lankford wasted no time in staking out five claims on February 20, 1891: the Robert E. Lee, the Blanche, the Hobo, the Panhandle, and the Blue Bell. Later, when George Carr was working on the Hobo claim in a gulch near the top of Guyot Hill he unearthed the grave of an Indian woman. This gulch was thereafter known as Squaw Gulch.

As the partners continued to work their mines, Spell purchased an ore wagon and four horses. Dick Dickerson was hired to haul the ore from Cripple Creek to Florissant, where it was then transferred to an ore car on the Midland Railroad and hauled to the smelter in Colorado City. Although the assays had promised about $175 a ton, this thirty-ton shipment only yielded a total of $1,930—about $64 a ton. It was the first and only ore shipment from Cripple Creek in 1891.

Ironically, Florissant carries the dubious honor of inadvertently inhibiting the same Cripple Creek boom that ultimately became one of the greatest in the world. Hiram Rogers, a reporter for the *Gazette*, wrote a story of a "very rich strike of gold" made near Florissant on February 12, 1891. The strike had been found by Captain J. H. Hensley on his ranch about a mile southeast of Florissant, just across the wagon road from the Florissant cemetery.

Atlanta (Long) Thompson worked for Mrs. Hensley during the previous year, 1890, while Captain Hensley was busy freighting to Leadville. Atlanta wrote that Mrs. Hensley was a woman about sixty years old, "overflowing with good nature and a pleasant word for everyone." She had fallen and broken her ankle, and needed help in managing her long, rambling log house. Captain and Mrs. Hensley also boarded many travelers, as their ranch was located along the Ute Pass Wagon Road, and Atlanta was expected to cook for them. Silas Thompson, Atlanta's future husband, and his sister Becca Nevitt together with her husband, Dan, also became boarders at the Hensley's in the early part of 1891.

When the Midland deposited Rogers, the *Gazette* reporter, in Florissant that February morning of 1891, he noted that the townsfolk were "not early risers. It was not until after 8 o'clock that the streets became at all inhabited, though they are not very lively at any stage of the game." Rogers finally found a group of ranchers, lumbermen and tie choppers gathered around the wood stove at Handbury & Lentz'. He noted that though they all talked of the mine at Hensley's, they were mostly inclined to be skeptical. Newcomers were dubiously questioned as to when and where they intended to stake their claims.

Rogers at last succeeded in finding a guide, and was escorted to the site by none other than "M.C. Langford" (our Marion Lankford) "who claimed to have had considerable mining experience, and who carried an old battered gold pan."

Rogers continued the story of his fact-finding trip to the "gold strike" in Florissant.

> ...After traveling on this road [Upper Twin Rock] perhaps half a mile [east], a thinly tenanted graveyard came into view on the south side of the road and directly opposite was a long, low log house, one story high, chinked up with mud in regulation style. At one side was a well and in front were two or three corrals,

house, one story high, chinked up with mud in regulation style. At one side was a well and in front were two or three corrals, through the lowered bars of which two cows are aimlessly meandering about. The mine, the natives said, was behind the house, so the three [of us] went through the yard and up about 200 yards from the house, where, on a hill-side a windlass and the top of a ladder could be seen above a pile of grayish broken stone. As the three [of us] came up a tall, very erect man, seemingly about 55 years old, with a long white beard, climbed the ladder bearing a basin full of a greenish gray stone. This was Captain J. H. Hensley, the discoverer of the vein...

The *Gazette* accorded Rogers a full three columns of details on Hensley's "strike." Rogers noted that about 150 claims had already been located in and around Florissant, the majority being in Hensley's potato patch. Rogers collected a sack of ore samples from Hensley's mine, and took it to Professor W.E. Strieby in Colorado Springs for a final analysis. Unfortunately, these tests showed that the metal "was beyond all doubt copper." In a final understatement, Rogers offers the insight that "the very decided opinion given by Prof. Strieby regarding the ore [from Hensley's] will put something of a damper on the boom..."

Ironically, Rogers concluded his story on the boom/bust at Florissant with the following paragraphs.

The talk about the find at Florissant brought to light a matter that the Gazette had promised to keep quiet until better developments gave it a foundation. This is the fact that a vein of gold ore has been found in the mountains and not a great way from Florissant. The story as told is as follows: About one month ago a young ranchman, [forty-six year old Bob Womack] rather well known in the city, came here with the statement that he had found a vein of rich ore. Very little attention was paid to it, but one citizen determined to look into the case.

...A Gazette representative was yesterday shown rock that it is claimed was taken from the vein and that it is alleged assays over $2200 to the ton...This find is about thirteen miles south of Florissant and not far from Mt. Pisgah, but is not in the red salted district. Developments will be awaited with interest.

This was the first that the public would know about the great gold strike that would change a nation. It was, however, overshadowed and undervalued because of the false excitement generated by Hensley's Florissant potato patch!

Florissant more than atoned for this slight derailment of Cripple's gold boom, nonetheless. This contribution came about as the result of having attracted and held one of the most beautiful women of the period, Berthe De Pourtales. (Count Louis Otto De Pourtales, her brother, was introduced earlier, in Chapter 6.)

Count Louis Otto's homestead north of Florissant provided a health-giving refuge for his recently divorced sister, Countess Berthe. Berthe, in turn, was the lovely magnet who compelled cousin Count James De Pourtales from his Prussian estates to Colorado Springs in 1884. By the fall of 1886, Count James and Countess Berthe had entered wedded bliss, and traveled to his estates in Glumbowitz, in Silesia—a region within what is now southwestern Poland. Count James' grandfather had made a fortune in the 1700s, and had dedicated his money and his allegiance to the Prussian King, who returned the favor by making Jacques Louis De Pourtales and his progeny counts and countesses.

CAPTAIN HENSLEY'S GOLD STRIKE resulted in a frenzy of mining activity around Florissant. Here Dr. Thomas A. McIntyre and CMRR engineer, Frank "Duffy" Malone, stand next to the observation platform built on top of Fortification Hill. McIntyre gained brief notoriety in 1915 when he wrote a prize-winning rebuttal to Julian Street's scathing *Collier's Weekly* article on Cripple Creek. *(Photo courtesy Carl Quist)*

Count James was an engaging, energetic man, with a creative, analytical mind. He determined that he could benefit from the boom he was sure would come to Palmer's fledgling Colorado Springs. When a friend gave him a tour of his struggling dairy farm, The Broadmoor, Count James was hooked. He bought a half interest, and then began a series of failed attempts to turn a profit on his $25,000 investment. Count James was a "big, cheery, positive, stubborn man who ate and drank and played and worked with gusto. He loved to think up bold schemes and to gamble his shirt on them." The Broadmoor proved a challenge worthy of such a man.

Broadmoor as a dairy farm met one catastrophe after another, and none of Count James' brilliant ideas nor thousands of dollars made a difference. Meanwhile, Colorado Springs was growing by leaps and bounds—from a mere 2,000 residents to over 8,000 in a little over five years. Count James therefore decided on a different course of action. From 1889 to 1890, he mortgaged the farm for $250,000 in order to develop it as Broadmoor City, boasting its own electric plant and water system. He planned and built the fabulous Broadmoor Casino as the crown jewel of his little town.

It was of no use. It seemed that a large black cloud of bad luck had stalled over the Broadmoor area and would not budge. With his Broadmoor investment at risk, and daily losing money, Count James was becoming desperate. And then came the rumors of gold at Cripple Creek. This news engendered thoughts for a different source of income. Everyone knew that Colorado's Rockies were full of gold and silver. In September of 1891, the Count boarded the Midland Railroad for Florissant. He then traveled the eighteen miles south to Cripple Creek in a rented buckboard, probably from Hundley's Florissant Livery.

What Count James found there could hardly have raised his hopes. "The Greatest Gold Camp on Earth" still consisted of Welty's log ranch house, a log store and a modest log hotel. Most of the would-be miners were simple cowboys from Florissant—William Spell, Marion Lankford, Sheriff Ed Bell, and Bob Womack—to name just a few. Nonetheless, Count James bought a few shares in a placer mine on Mineral Hill. He then returned to Colorado Springs after only two days of inspection.

In November, however, Count James returned to Cripple Creek with his friend Tom Parrish. They stayed with George and Emma Carr who now leased the Welty ranch. Emma was thoroughly charmed by the Count, and gave him the "bed of honor"—on the kitchen table. Making breakfast the next morning proved a challenge worthy of Emma, who simply moved the snoring Count's feet apart in order to roll out her biscuit dough. In return for their hospitality, the Count regaled his hosts with lusty renditions of arias from *Fidelio*.

Pourtales and Parrish remained in Cripple Creek a little over a week this time. They inspected Stratton's Independence Mine and several others. Count James had hired an Aspen mining expert, Wolcott Newberry, as his technical adviser. Ironically, Newberry, the expert, advised him to steer clear of the Independence, and instead invest in the Buena Vista on Bull Hill. Mining at Cripple Creek was different from most other gold mines. This fact had escaped most experts, including Newberry, and it was one of the main reasons that Cripple was so difficult to develop. Cripple's floor is composed mainly of Cripple Creek Granite, created by a giant bubble of magma which cooled beneath the surface and whose pale pink color is the result of feldspar.

Eventually, there was a great eruption of volcanic material through this more ancient granite. As this hot magma cooled, solidified and contracted, large fissures were formed. Still seething, the subterranean volcano now forced hot water through these fissures. As this water cooled and stagnated, it deposited vast amounts of minerals, and these precipitated the formation of gold.

Cripple's volcanic rock is mainly andesite breccia—commonly known as porphyry because of its deep purple color. The ores from this rock are tellurides, calaverite, and sylvanite, which were barely known in America at the time. They were, however, very common to the gold mines in Count Pourtales' Transylvania. Cripple's miners later discovered that the gold from these ores quickly revealed itself when heated in a hot frying pan.

News of Count Pourtales' investment in Cripple Creek was splashed across the *Gazette* on November 10, 1891. This proved to be the seminal event in the history of the gold camp. Count James was one of the more glamorous members of Little London's social set, due, no doubt, to his title, his estates in Prussia, and his engaging manner. Whatever Count James did, the rest of Springs society tried to emulate. Suddenly Cripple Creek exploded with rich bankers and playboys from Denver and Colorado Springs.

Unfortunately for Count James, the Pikes Peak area still held that large, black financial cloud. In 1896, the count had to liquidate all of his mining interests and the Broadmoor City. He realized a net loss of over $200,000.

Spencer Penrose ultimately bought the Broadmoor, where he and Julie built their mansion. Under Penrose's guidance, lots sold like proverbial hotcakes, and the Broadmoor Hotel became one of the world's premiere luxury resorts. Stratton's spurned Independence Mine sold for eleven million dollars. James J. Hagerman, who had bought controlling interest in the Count's Buena Vista mine, became one of the wealthiest men in Colorado Springs. Count James

Chapter VIII

COUNTESS BERTHE DE POURTALES, a former Florissant resident. Her beauty proved an instrument of fate for Cripple Creek. Without her, Count James Pourtales may never have come to Colorado, and there may never have been an investor willing to risk money in the new Cripple Creek Mining District. *(Photo courtesy Colorado Springs Pioneer Museum)*

had the Midas touch. Unfortunately, however, it seemed to have a delayed reaction and benefited only those who came after him. Nonetheless, without his involvement, Cripple Creek may very well have died on the vine for want of investors.

Happily, Count James was willing to gamble again—this time on the Commonwealth mine in Pearce, Arizona. His share of the thirty million dollars produced by this mine allowed him and his beautiful Berthe to return to his estates in Prussia in grand style, where they then remained.

When Count James became involved in Cripple Creek, the groundwork had already been

218

laid for the boom by those "erstwhile" Florissant cowboys lounging around Welty's ranch house. Most miners vividly recalled the debacle at Tarryall some thirty years before. In 1859, a few greedy miners staked out every claim available in the Tarryall region, precluding latecomers from participating in the strike. These unfortunate men derisively called the strike "Grab-all," and were careful to fairly organize the next strike which they thoughtfully named Fairplay. Similarly, Florissant's cowboys wanted to ensure a fair playing field for all miners in Cripple Creek.

Appropriate and fair organization of a new mining district was vital to Cripple Creek's development. United States laws were very liberal in allowing miners to establish their special districts themselves. When Bob Womack rode the Midland from the Springs to Florissant in late February, 1891, he met Ed De La Vergne and his partner who had just returned from staking claims adjacent to his in Cripple Creek. Womack seemed overwhelmed that his prophecies of gold in Cripple Creek were at last validated by others. He remained in Florissant for another three days, sleeping on the sugar sacks in Frank Castello's Florissant Mercantile.

Captain Hensley's Florissant potato patch had temporarily overshadowed Womack's gold strike, so poor old Bob was met with derision and skepticism while in Colorado Springs. Florissant was a different matter, however. Some dozen or so Florissant residents had already staked their claims, led by Womack's old mentor, Lankford. Womack now luxuriated around the pot bellied stove in Castello's Mercantile, as his entourage of future millionaires talked excitedly of Cripple. It was decided that a proper mining district must be organized as soon as practicable. Frank Castello assumed command, and announced a meeting date of April 5 at the Carr's Broken Box Ranch.

George and Emma Carr were always delighted at the prospect of having visitors. Emma was one of those most remarkable ranch women who seemed capable of doing anything, and doing it well. She spent the three days prior to the miner's meeting cleaning house and baking pies for her guests. Leslie and Oakley Doyle (Doy) Spell, Bill Spell's children, recalled their admiration for Mrs. Carr in their book *Forgotten Men of Cripple Creek.*

> ...We especially enjoyed watching Mrs. Carr gracefully riding sidesaddle, weaving in and out among the cattle, cutting them out as wanted. We admired the dexterity with which she handled her horse, for she was an accomplished horsewoman and made a striking appearance with the flowing skirt of her riding habit, her auburn hair tucked neatly under the mannish hat she wore. Mrs. Carr keenly enjoyed her part in helping with the roundup, but didn't neglect her obligations as hostess and made our visit a most pleasant one. No matter how busy, she was always gracious and hospitable—the true gentle-woman.

Cripple's first miner's meeting was held on Sunday, April 5th, 1891, as scheduled. Castello arrived early from Florissant, leading three mules laden with refreshments from his store. Bill Spell served as temporary chairman, and opened the meeting held around a bonfire on the hillside next to the Carr's ranch. Fifteen of Florissant's cowboys were present, outnumbering the other prospective millionaires. George Carr was elected chairman, and a committee was formed to write camp rules and regulations. The name "Cripple Creek Mining

District" beat the name "Womack Mining District" by only a few votes.

Cripple Creek had been named by Levi Welty who had been ranching in the area since 1871. Welty built a house and corrals near a little stream that ran down the valley, below the current townsite. (Welty's homestead later became the Broken Box Ranch, leased by George Carr from the owners, Horace Bennett and Julius Myers.) Early on, one of the Welty boys fell off the roof and broke his arm. Another of the boys cut his foot while chopping wood. Their hired man, Ben Roberts, set out to pack some bear meat to one of the roundup camps when his horse got a whiff, began to buck and then stepped in a prairie dog hole, breaking both his leg and his rider's leg. All of these misfortunes caused the Welty's to proclaim that "that sure was one cripple creek!" The name stuck, and has been used since that day, in spite of several attempts at other names.

This new mining district, Cripple Creek, was six miles square, or about 23,000 acres. Rules were very liberal. Anyone could file a lode claim, 1500 feet long and 300 feet wide— about ten acres. All that was required was to set six location stakes, tell El Paso's county clerk about it and perform $100 of labor on the claim each year. Prospect holes were designated by placing a pick and a shovel at the entrance as evidence of possession.

Bill Spell was appointed Camp Marshal, mainly because he already held the office of El Paso County deputy sheriff. Marshall Spell was also pressed into service as the recorder of mining claims, and spent many long nights laboriously making entries in the district's leather-bound ledger while seated at the kitchen table of his Florissant home.

By 1893, the fledgling mining district had grown sufficiently that the records were kept in an office on Bennett Avenue. However, Cripple's disastrous fires of 1896 destroyed all of these carefully kept records. Cripple's miners were therefore required to make affidavits as to the date and location of their claims. To this day, there are numerous duplications and errors in the mines, which were recorded in the fire's aftermath.

Most of the real money in a gold mining camp is made by anyone astute enough to understand a miner's basic need for sustenance. This is easily reflected in the use of the term "grub stake." Cripple Creek was not exempt from this rule. Cripple's population grew exponentially as word of the gold strike spread. Shortly after the first district meeting at the Carr Ranch in April, 1891, there were about 450 prospectors in the district. By the next year, their ranks had swollen to a hefty 2,500. By 1893, there were easily 12,500! By the turn of the century, the bowl of Cripple's ancient volcano resembled a beehive of activity as 50,000 people searched for the golden needles in her granite haystack.

Frank Castello was easily poised for profit with his tidy little mercantile store in Florissant. Until 1894, Florissant was the main route for gold seekers, tourists, and ore haulers from and to Cripple Creek. Colorado Spring's *Gazette* reported on Florissant's newly found prosperity in a story on February 2nd, 1892.

> Florissant, one of the prettiest and best located little towns
> in El Paso county had several booms, but none of them have ever
> succeeded in raising the town much above the level of a

lumberman's center. Since the Cripple Creek excitement Florissant has been the chief railroad point for the new camp and the majority of the travel has gone that way. Many people are of the opinion that the metropolis of Twin Creek will continue to be the main supply point for the gold mines. Be this as it may, its beautiful location and the fact that it may some day be a county seat give Florissant a strong claim on the future.

Florissant's John Hundley operated the first stage line from Florissant to Cripple Creek. Fifteen six-horse stages met the daily demand for transportation to the gold camps. Miners, supplies, and U.S. Mail were all hauled up Ute Pass aboard the Colorado Midland Railroad, where they were unloaded at Florissant. Miners who had not yet outfitted themselves wandered into Castello's store or Handbury & Lentz' mercantile, bought pick, shovel, tent, coffee, beans and flour. Those that could afford Hundley's ten dollar fare then climbed aboard the Concord for a rollicking ride to the gold camp.

Mrs. Nellie S. Pyles of Florissant was a passenger on the first stage to Cripple Creek. She later told C.S. Dudley of the *Gazette Telegraph* that "there was fear the stage might slide off the road, so at places all the men but the driver got out and pushed on it to keep it from going sideways, and she was the only passenger in it." (Nellie and her husband, Thomas Benton Pyles, published the first newspaper on the west slope of the Peak. Unfortunately, no copies of the *Crystal Peak Beacon* have ever been located. Their paper was printed in Florissant from 1889 until 1894.)

Hundley's Concord stages were usually packed with those seeking their fortune in the new-found gold fields. Many of the Concords were equipped with an additional center row of seats which folded down when not in use. Needless to say, packing six to nine adults into this cramped space sometimes proved an overly interesting experience. One of these early travelers noted his experience on just such a packed stage coach.

This gentleman was already aboard when a rather heavy-set woman, in voluminous skirts, boarded. After a prolonged, uncomfortable silence the gentleman finally asked the new passenger if she would kindly consent to "dovetail" with him. Dovetailing was a common means of affording everyone comfort. This was done by interlacing the facing passenger's legs from the two opposing seats. This very proper lady had obviously never encountered the term before, however, and soundly slapped her facing partner, the offending gentleman. She also demanded that the driver discharge her at the next stop, where she fled the coach in an indignant huff!

Most passengers vied for the very best seat on the stage. This was up front, in the open air, next to the driver. The scenery from this vantage point was usually spectacular. It was considered a great honor when the driver allowed one onto the coveted seat next to him.

Demand for stagecoaches and freight hauling made the entire venture a lucrative one. By the close of 1892, there were three stage lines into Cripple Creek—Hundley's, Montgomery's, and Welty's. By the winter of 1893, three more stage lines offered their services. In the spring of 1893, a toll road was opened from Hayden's Divide into Cripple Creek. Hundley then expanded his operations to include a coach which met the Midland at Divide, and carried its passengers down the new toll road on an even more perilous ride to the gold camp.

Over eight thousand pounds of express were tugged daily up the two thousand foot climb from Florissant to Cripple. Ore wagons were pressed into service in hauling food stuffs and equipment to the miners, returning with loads of gold ore for the Midland Railroad to haul to Manitou Springs for processing.

Remarkably, there were few thefts of this precious gold ore. Adeline Hornbek's son, Elliot, was one of the first stage drivers. He reported to C.S. Dudley of the *Gazette Telegraph* that it "was usually kept a secret just when the most valuable ore was to be brought down and that, strange as it may seem, he cannot remember that there were any holdups or robberies."

Dudley goes on to describe (in the *Gazette Telegraph*) the boom that came to Florissant in those early days of Cripple Creek madness.

> ...Florissant was the jumping-off place for the Cripple Creek district before a railroad was built to Cripple Creek [in 1894]. Gold seekers went to Florissant by rail and then made their way, first on foot, then by stage, to the land of prospects. Up the Florissant-Cripple Creek road toiled six and eight-horse teams with wagons loaded with provisions and vast amounts of machinery and other mining equipment. Down the road came these same wagons filled with ore, sometimes a single load valued at thousands of dollars. This ore was shipped over the Midland railroad to Colorado City, now west of Colorado Springs, for treatment. Things happened so fast, and there was so much activity, in Florissant in the 1890's that it is difficult to imagine the picture of the town, now an agricultural and stock-raising center, as the mining town of those romantic days described by old residents.
>
> Gold was not found at Florissant, but for several years

Florissant was the door out of which Cripple Creek's golden stream poured, and the stories of fortunes made almost overnight, and of the telling, as something of new interest loomed up ahead.

Castello's Florissant Mercantile not only proved a virtual gold mine for its owner, but it also paved the way in making Frank Castello one of Cripple's first millionaires.

Richard Houghton, a kindly man with a fondness for liquor, homesteaded about three-quarters of a mile north of Florissant on the East Oil Creek Trail (now Wildhorn Road) about 1884. Houghton, like many other veterans, used his Civil War experience to take advantage of the special homestead provisions accorded them. Although plagued with a permanent limp from his war duty, he developed his homestead into a small dairy with about a dozen milk cows. Florissant's growing populace relished "Uncle" Dick's supply of sweet, fresh milk, cream and cheeses. This income, coupled with his small government pension, provided a modest living for him, his wife and four children.

Dairy farming is a severe task master, however, and is especially so in Colorado's Rockies. It is not unusual for frigid winter nights to dip to thirty and forty below zero. Uncle Dick's hands became cracked, red and rough, as did those of his beautiful Mary. Cows had to be milked twice daily no matter what the temperature. William Spell's children, Leslie Doyle (Doy) and Hazel, later fondly recalled Mary McKinney Houghton in their book *Forgotten Men of Cripple Creek.*

...Mrs. Houghton, nee Mary McKinney, was a woman beloved of the entire community. Doubtless when younger, she was a beautiful woman. However, at the time I, as a lad of six or seven, knew her first, her beauty had faded in a physical way with the years of toil and responsibility of rearing a family, as well as caring for a husband who sometimes drifted home in a drunken stupor. She never lost patience with Uncle Dick for his faults, often undressing and putting him to bed with no words of recrimination. To my childish eyes, she was still beautiful. I have pleasant memories of the many times she would lift me onto her homemade kitchen stool and offer a glass of milk and cookies from her well-filled cookie jar when I appeared at her door with a pail for our family's supply of milk...It was Mrs. Houghton's task to milk the cows and care for the milk. Her hands were calloused, the knuckles misshapen from hard work, but gentle as a fairy's when lifting me to the stool.

Uncle Dick was a valued member of the community, and served as chairman for Florissant's school district. It was mainly through his efforts that the new well-constructed, two-room school was built in Florissant in 1887. Nonetheless, Houghton hoped for a better life for his family, and assuaged the pain of his wounded ambitions in cheap whiskey.

Houghton and his sons, John and Haddon, had acquired a smattering of knowledge about mining and had half-heartedly picked at the rose-colored granite around Florissant. They, too, were skeptical of most claims—having first-hand experience of the hoaxes at Mount Pisgah and at Hensley's potato patch. However, two separate events worked to change Uncle Dick's mind.

First, his friend Frank Castello filed two separate claims in Cripple with Houghton's brother, Tom, in early May. Then, he actually saw Dick Dickerson hauling wagon after wagon of ore from Spell & Carr's Blue Bell Mine into Florissant. In late spring of 1891, he could restrain himself no longer. He and his boys loaded their wagon with a camping outfit and headed for Cripple Creek.

On the north end of Guyot Hill, Uncle Dick found a small ravine where the ravages of nature had revealed a well-defined vein of blue fluorine quartz. Uncle Dick knew enough of mining to understand that this quartz was a pretty sure indicator of gold. Excitedly, he panned some of the gravel, and as suspected, found tiny flecks of gold. He wasted no time in locating his claim on that fateful day in late May of 1891, barely seven months after Womack's momentous find in nearby Poverty Gulch. At last he would be able to give his wife the life that she so deserved. In her honor, then, he named his claim the Mary McKinney.

Uncle Dick and his sons worked their placer for over a year while Mary ran their Florissant dairy. Finally, he became discouraged. Only three mines were able to produce ore throughout 1891. Even after Count Pourtales validated the Strike in Cripple Creek with his investment, there were only about fifty mines shipping ore up to the Colorado Midland Railroad in Florissant by the fall of 1892. Unfortunately, Uncle Dick did not have the wherewithal to continue working his claim and support his family. Also, Mary's health was failing, and he was needed back at his farm. He abandoned his work on the mine and returned to Florissant.

There still was the matter of his grub stake at Castello's mercantile, however. During the year he spent searching for his fortune in Cripple's crater, he had run up a $30.00 grocery bill at Castello's—equivalent to about one month's wages. Castello felt sorry for his old friend, and agreed to accept title to the Mary McKinney in exchange for Uncle Dick's indebtedness.

Later, Castello was commiserating with his friend, J.P. Ryan, about having accepted the "worthless" mining claim in lieu of cash. Ryan, a telegraph agent for the Colorado Midland Railroad, was smitten. He offered Castello his life savings, $30.00, for a half interest in the claim. Neither Castello nor Ryan had the several thousand dollars needed to develop the Mary McKinney, so they decided to lease the claim. After several years and as many different lessees, Castello and Ryan finally formed their own mining company in 1895. The Mary McKinney soon became one of Cripple's top producers, cashing in on over $11,000,000 in gold! Frank Castello became a multi-millionaire at the age of 44.

William Spell's son, Doy, worked at the Mary McKinney and noted with pride that the "setup and the management was the acme of efficiency. There was a saying around the camp at one time if a man wanted a job at the Mary McKinney mine he would need wait for someone to die, as workman turnover was unusual."

Atlanta (Long) Thompson recalled in her book *Daughter of a Pioneer* that Houghton did not end up penniless from his mining venture. Her version of Castello's grub stake differs slightly from that of Spell.

> ...A man by the name of Houghton stumbled over there and staked the Mary McKiney [sic] mine, naming it for his wife's maiden name. He was a man who was seldom sober, but drunk or sober he was always talking about Mary. Poor Mary had a large family and if it hadn't been for Frank Castillo [sic], merchant in

Florissant who let them have groceries, they would have starved to death. Houghton came home from Cripple Creek the first winter there had been any prospecting done there, and went to Frank Castillo [sic] and asked him how much he owed him. When Frank told him fifteen hundred dollars, Houghton replied, "I haven't any money Frank, but I am sure I have a mine, and I will give you an interest in it." This interest afterward made Frank a wealthy man. Houghton later sold his share for fifty thousand dollars. He then took poor Mary, who was hardly able to walk around, to Denver and put her under the care of the best doctor, while he took the Keeley cure. Mary had a cancer and lived only a year. Houghton stopped at our house on his way home from Colorado Springs, soon after he discovered his mine, to show me a gorgeous hat he had bought for Mary. It was an elaborate affair with quantities of red roses on the crown and when he asked me if I didn't think Mary would like it, I could hardly keep from smiling. I assured him that I knew she would, but I couldn't picture poor, plain, Mary wearing it.

Fifteen years later, Doy Spell chanced to travel to the Old Soldier's Home in Monte Vista, south of Florissant in the San Luis Valley. Doy recalled his poignant encounter with Uncle Dick in *Forgotten Men of Cripple Creek.*

…While walking down the street there I noticed an old man sitting on a bench who looked strangely familiar. I stopped and said: "Hello, Uncle Dick." He looked up quickly. I grabbed his hand and shook it, but he didn't recognize me until I told him who I was. Then he quavered: "Of course, Doy, I remember you, Doy Spell." He asked about father, mother, and our family, and then told of his. His daughters had married, his boys were working as foremen of the ore sorting crew at the Mary McKinney. We talked long of Cripple Creek, Florissant, and of the schoolhouse he had built. After reminiscing for about two hours it was time for me to leave. Uncle Dick's lower lip began to quiver and tears spilled over. I walked along the street for a short distance, then looked back to wave. He was still watching me.

Initially, Cripple Creek's unique type of gold ore was very easily, and quite frequently, found near the surface. For this reason, it became known as the "poor man's gold camp." Many of the mines were worked with a simple farmer's plow, which churned up rich volcanic float laden with gold. A young carpenter from Florissant was one of these fortunate "gold farmers." Matthew Sterrett had joined Castello, Spell, and Carr in the early excitement and in organizing the Cripple Creek District. He then located his "Pride of the Rockies" in April of 1891, and then the more lucrative "Deer Horn Lode" in May of 1891. Atlanta (Long) Thompson recalled that Sterrett harvested over "twelve thousand dollars worth of ore at grass roots" from his Deer Horn Lode.

Miss Sarah Elizabeth (Sally) Halthusen, Herman's daughter, (who was briefly mentioned earlier) found her own unique way of mining for Cripple's gold. She moved from her father's Florissant ranch down to a house on Bennett Avenue, in Cripple Creek. She took most of her rogue horses with her so that she could continue with her hobby of breaking them. Somehow, Sally had managed to capture the attention of Spencer Penrose. And Spencer was enamored with this big-busted, high-spirited horse woman. He even ignored the fact that she had collected ransom from a Denver family in exchange for breaking her engagement to their son. Spencer's blue-blooded father was much alarmed at this romance, however. So Dr. Penrose sent Dick

BENNETT AVENUE, CRIPPLE CREEK circa 1897. The brick building on the left is the Bell Brothers Building, now home of the Cripple Creek Police Department. This seems appropriate, since Bell was originally the Sheriff of Florissant before moving to Cripple Creek in the 1890s. *(Photo courtesy Ute Pass Historical Society)*

Penrose to Cripple to talk some sense into his brother.

This approach seems to have been successful, and prevented the smitten Spencer from making Miss Sally into Mrs. Penrose. Sally, however, was a mite touchy about the entire episode. She severely beat a young chambermaid whose loose tongue detailed the affair in Sally's hearing. Sally was therefore hauled into court where she was found guilty of assault and fined $10 plus costs. In 1895, Sally healed her broken heart by marrying Thomas Gough, Jr., a hotel owner. When her father died in 1903, Sally and her siblings waged a legal battle against his widow—their stepmother—for possession of the estate.

A few miles south of the Halthusen Ranch, Reverend David Long (Atlanta Thompson's father) established a homestead on the road to Cripple Creek when he returned to the area in 1877. Reverend Long regularly corresponded with his favorite niece, Julia Snare. Julia and her husband Charles had settled on a sod farm in southwestern Kansas where the "land was as level as a floor." Their farm never raised a thing but large clods of dirt, and so Reverend Long encouraged them to come to Colorado.

Long's optimism about the prospects of Pikes Peak backcountry was no doubt based on the boom in nearby Cripple Creek. Farmers and ranchers in the area faced more demand for their goods than they could possibly supply. Julia and Charles sold their Kansas sod farm for $5, packed their few belongings in a covered wagon with a four horse team, then headed for Pikes Peak on April 10, 1895. Julia's first two infant daughters had died within their first year of life, and she was anxious about her thirteen-month-old son Claude Maxwell. She fretted over the wind and rain and snow that plagued them as they followed the old Santa Fe Trail into Colorado. When they arrived in Pueblo twelve days later, the baby was quite sick.

Julia's (unpublished) journal reflects her anxiety as they turned north from Pueblo on April 23rd. "Started out in good time, bad roads and horses hard to get along. Did not get quite to Fountain, we stopped several places to get bread, as we are out, finally got a small loaf. Baby still sick." When they arrived in Fountain the next day, the horses had to be re-shod and the wagon break fixed. Julia traded her rug-making machine to the blacksmith and his wife in return for their services, and then she, Charles and the baby resumed their journey to the mountains. As they began their ascent of Ute Pass, Julia wrote that the area afforded "grand scenery and narrow roads"—perfectly reflecting her gift for understatement.

They arrived at "Uncle Dave's" at dusk on April 26th, sixteen grueling days after leaving their home in Mead, Kansas. Reverend Long helped them settle into their new ranch near Sheep Rock, on what is now Mueller State Park. Charles wasted no time in planting potatoes and seed oats, while Julia made furniture for their new home, cooked, sewed, and tended the baby.

In these early days of ranching, the government allowed an individual to fence as much land as he cared to, provided he didn't enclose it. Most ranchers took advantage of this practice, running the open end of their fenced ranch up against a mountain, a gulch or any other handy obstacle that would effectively "close" the required opening. In this manner, anyone with a small patch of farm land or a homestead could easily expand into ranching without having to purchase the required acreage.

The Snares' new neighbors to the east were the notorious horse rustlers, the White Brothers (mentioned in Chapter 6). Julia notes in her journal on May 24th that "a man [was] here hunting for his horses." But that was life in the west. It was usually best to mind your own business, and just let the other fellow be. The financial opportunities afforded by the geography of the region were not always legal.

Over fifty years later, Julia's son Walter Nathan, "Nate," wrote about his mother.

My mother really liked the mountains, they were doing real good. Had their homestead, built a two-room log cabin and later got enough lumber to build a nice addition. This frame part was painted which was rare in those days, here in this part of Colorado. Of course the gold mines were booming in Cripple Creek, which made a ready market for things they might have to sell. Also sawmills were numberous [sic], and my Dad worked at them when times were slack.

Nate had an older sister, Alice Ione, who died in 1901 from scarlet fever, two years before he was born. His parents were distraught over the death of their beautiful five-year-old daughter. They were especially grieved that they had been unable to find a doctor in the area to attend to her, and who could perhaps have prevented her death. So Charles and Julia loaded their two surviving children, Max and Wayne, into the wagon and headed to Kirksville, Missouri where Charles studied to become a doctor. He received his Doctor of Osteopathy in 1905.

Pikes Peak backcountry had taken hold of their hearts, however, and they longed to return. The opportunity finally presented itself in 1914, and Max, now nineteen years old, and his seventeen-year-old brother Wayne were sent back to their Pikes Peak ranch to prepare it for the rest of the family. Tragically, their father passed away on the day before Christmas. Their mother wired them from Kansas to dig a grave for their father, that she was bringing him home to bury him. The two teenagers then spent Christmas day digging a hole six-foot deep in the frozen ground. Julia returned on December 27th, 1914 and buried her husband. In the tradition of Adeline Hornbek, she and the two older boys successfully ranched, raising her three youngest children, aged 11, 8 and 6 in the shadow of Sheep Rock.

235

DR. CHARLES SNARE'S WIDOW, JULIA, AND FOUR OF HER FIVE CHILDREN shortly after her **husband's death.** This photo was taken at their homestead cabin near Sheep Rock (now Mueller State Park). (L-R) Wayne Snare, Julia Snare, Dorothy Snare, Nate Snare, Hanna Long (Julia's sister), Charles Snare, Hazel Long (Julia's sister-in-law, married to John Long), and little Julia Long (Hazel's daughter). *(Photo courtesy Rose White, Dorothy Snare's daughter)*

Dr. Charles Snare never lived to see his beloved homestead again, but his sons established a virtual ranching dynasty on the west slope of Pikes Peak. Max, the oldest son, built the family ranch into a prosperous outfit along the banks of Hay Creek (originally called East Oil Creek) which he later sold for $4 an acre to a man named Dwain Werley (or Worley). His ranch is now part of Mueller State Park. The youngest son, Charles Julian, took advantage of the revised Homestead Act of 1916 and filed on thousands of acres of ranch land south of the entrance to what is now Mueller Park and several sections surrounding Dome Rock. His ranch is also now part of Mueller State Park.

One of the middle sons, Walter Nathan or "Nate," ranched along the southern border of what is now the Florissant Fossil Beds National Monument. In private correspondence, Nate noted that nearly all the ranchers in the area "were thin-hipped and broad shouldered and their faces were sunburned." He also noted that many of them ran "old Texas long-horned cattle. They were just hides stretched over the bones, and horns three feet long."

In 1904, a prominent Cripple Creek banker, John Delano Husted, organized the Crescent Cattle Company. The company was organized as a ranching enterprise, and sold its stock primarily to religious ministers in the Boston area. Crescent Cattle Company purchased large sections of grazing land from Divide down to the Four Mile area. Headquarters for the Ranch was established just west of Divide, but the real business of the ranch was conducted by the stockholders during the summer at an elaborate "cabin" called Jack Rabbit Lodge. It is even rumored that Teddy Roosevelt was a guest here during a hunting trip to the Pikes Peak area.

In the early 1950s, W.E. Mueller began purchasing the fragments of what had been Crescent Cattle Company land (they had gone bankrupt in 1924). After a twenty-year stint of ranching the area, Mueller approached The Nature Conservancy in the early 1970s. He hoped to sell his property in a way that would protect its beauty and wildlife from the press of development.

The Conservancy purchased the ranch in 1978, and then sold it to the State of Colorado in 1980. Mueller State Park was officially opened to the public in August of 1991. Today, visitors can hike along the Park's 90 miles of trail, enjoying glimpses of elk, big horn sheep, mule deer, eagles, hawks and song birds. The Park also affords breathtaking views of Pikes Peak, the Sangre de Cristos, and some of the collegiate Peaks.

"Always a bride's maid, never a bride!" might well be applied to the fate of little Florissant. Cripple Creek promised prosperity for the little town, but it came with a whimper rather than a shout. At the peak of the gold strike in the late 1800s, Florissant boasted no more than 300 residents. Eventually, however, three sets of rails were laid into Cripple, which all but negated ore shipments on the Colorado Midland from Florissant. Most of the ore was instead routed through Hayden's Divide via the Midland Terminal Line, built into Cripple in 1895. The breathtakingly beautiful Short Line Railroad was built from the Broadmoor area, south around Pikes Peak and into Victor and Cripple in April, 1901. This became the preferred route for sightseers and business men traveling to the gold camps. Some sightseers still came through Florissant on the Midland, but only to harvest her still abundant wildflowers and fossils.

Unfortunately, Florissant's new millionaires were not bound to her by her beauty. Frank Castello sold his mercantile to William Allen, and moved to a fancy house in Colorado Springs in 1898. Marshall Ed Bell moved to Cripple in 1896, where he and his brother built their Bennett Avenue-First Street Building. They became real estate brokers as well as stock brokers. Ed Bell later became Teller County Sheriff in 1899 when the county was carved out of El Paso County. Fittingly, his old offices now house the Cripple Creek Police Department.

Frank Burnham sold his Twin Creek Ranch to Charles Sisler in 1899. Allen then continued the tradition of Castello's Mercantile by grub staking Sisler as he searched for his fortune in Cripple Creek. Two years later, Sisler defaulted on his grub stake, turning over the title of his beautiful Twin Creek Ranch to Allen for "One dollar and other good & valuable consideration." Allen and his family then plied their excellent carpentry skills and built the lovely Victorian ranch house at the Twin Creek Ranch in 1904.

Adding insult to injury, Florissant even lost her favorite fiddle player, Kale Wilson. Kale had courted Atlanta Long some time before she married Silas Thompson. Atlanta described him as "a lazy sort of fellow but really good company." Others weren't so kind, describing him as a fellow that was "too lazy to live." Nonetheless, Kale found his way down to Cripple where he staked a claim. When a friend of his happened to pass by, he asked him "Why, Kale, what are you digging there for? There is no vein or float there." Kale replied that the spot was chosen because "this big tree makes it shady." Atlanta wrote that her phlegmatic old beau actually did strike gold there in the grass roots, and made a nice tidy fortune. Florissant's barn dances were never the same, however.

As the new-found gold began to drain the life from Florissant, it also infused life into Cripple Creek, which then gave birth to its neighbor, Victor. Locals deridingly called the gold seekers "coffee coolers" in reference to their habit of digging a little bit, then sitting and waiting for their coffee to cool enough to drink it. Cowboys in the area complained about one particular "coffee cooler" who had dug a hole right in the middle of one of their cattle trails at the base of Bull Hill. They kept him supplied in fresh meat, however, in hopes that he would cover up

his hole when he was done. This inconvenient hole turned out the be the $14 million dollar

Independence Mine, and the prospector was none other than Winfield Scott Stratton.

Four hundred feet west of Stratton's Independence Mine, an ex-teamster named J.R.

McKinnie staked out the Black Diamond Mine and the Mount Rosa Placer. In fact, it was

McKinnie—a "jolly, pink-cheeked Santa Claus of a man"—who had befriended Stratton on his

first visit into the Cripple Creek District in May of 1891. In 1893, McKinnie sold his 136-acre

Mount Rosa Placer to two "quiet, mousy, ardent Baptists," Frank and Harry Woods, for $1000.

The Woods brothers shrewdly laid out a townsite on their new mine, and called it Victor.

They chose the name in honor of the original homesteader of the adjacent Lawrence townsite,

Victor C. Adams. In a burst of Cripple Creek fever, the Woods boys sold their town lots by

telling prospective buyers that every lot was a potential gold mine. Lots sold so well that the

brothers next decided to build the Victor Hotel. However, while Frank Woods was grading the

lot for the hotel, he struck a twenty-inch vein of gold. He traced the vein to its source, the Gold

Coin, which he quietly and quickly purchased for a few thousand dollars. In a very short time,

the Gold Coin was earning $50,000 a month for its new owners.

Of course, Victor grew by leaps and bounds as owners of the town lots saw the promise

of gold in their midst. Subterranean Victor kept pace with the township above. Vast timbered

tunnels soon connected the Gold Coin, the Strong and dozens of other mines. It was possible

to walk, underground, the entire distance from Victor to Cripple Creek. Since these shafts lay

VICTOR, COLORADO IN THE LATE 1800s. Nestled at the base of Bull Hill, Victor was officially born as a town in 1893. Winfield S. Stratton, Cripple Creek Mining District's first, and most eccentric, millionaire lived in a small, modest house near his Independence Mine. Cripple Creek Mining District is now a National Historic District, with many of its historic buildings and mines as they were 100 years ago. *(Photo courtesy Ute Pass Historical Society)*

underneath the town itself, they soon became a haven for criminals. These cunning men came to know this labyrinth of underground streets and put them to good use. Victor became the capital of crime, although when it incorporated in 1894, it billed itself as The City of Mines.

When labor disputes erupted in Cripple Creek and Victor in the mid-1890s, hundreds of miners left for greener pastures. Many of these men traveled thirty miles west, past McIntyre Mountain (made notorious by the Mount Pisgah hoax of 1884). They sunk their picks and

GUFFEY, COLORADO IN THE EARLY 1900s. Guffey's City Hall commands the left edge of this photo. George West drives the team while Amos Hardy plows Guffey's main street. *(Photo courtesy Maud Marie & Maurice Ownbey)*

shovels into the surface of an extinct volcano in the Freshwater Mining District. This District earned its name by virtue of two gulches; one carved by a soda water spring, or Soda Water Gulch, and the other by—of course—a fresh water spring. In January of 1896, the town of Freshwater was incorporated based on a townsite survey by Will C. Teller.

"Idaville" was the name originally given to the post office in April, 1895. It was named in honor of Ida McClavey Wagner who owned the mining claims on Gold Hill, which towers above the townsite on the north. However, when street improvements were needed in town the

FRONTIER JUSTICE, GUFFEY STYLE. This two-cell jail was built around 1900 after a local rancher was murdered. It is very clear that prisoners enjoyed few privileges. *(Photo courtesy Helen Cahill)*

following year, James McClurg Guffey provided the funding. In gratitude, the 500 citizens of the town voted to rename the town "Guffey" in May of 1896, in honor of their benefactor. There were no great gold strikes to ensure Guffey's place in history. Many miners, however, still contend that the mother lode of Cripple Creek lies hidden under Guffey's Gold Hill. Guffey remains notorious in recent times, nonetheless, for her penchant for electing four-footed mayors. After a series of cats, the most recent Mayor is a lovely and loveable golden retriever.

None of Cripple's gold seemed to stick in Teller County. Her total production has been estimated at about $450 million dollars—placing her in fifth place world wide. By the early

1900s, Florissant was once again a sleepy little cow town, and Cripple fell into a similar fate. Prosperity had been shipped out by the trainload, and like both Cripple's and Florissant's trains, it soon disappeared.

A different, and perhaps more stable economy, has now come to Pikes Peak backcountry in the form of the Florissant Fossil Beds National Monument and Mueller State Park. Limited gaming has been introduced into Cripple Creek, and Woodland Park and Divide have become bedroom communities for Colorado Springs. There had been an exciting moment, however, once upon a time in their past. As Robert Service wrote, "...it isn't the gold that I'm wanting, so much as just finding the gold."

CHAPTER IX: THE PETRIFIED FOREST

Fortunately, gold of a more lasting and, perhaps, more enriching nature was buried in the hills surrounding Florissant. Ute Indians, marveling at the dark outlines of fossilized images in the pale-gold shale, allegedly named Florissant the "Valley of the Shadows."

Early trappers, returning to Taos from the beaver rich streams surrounding Florissant, reported on the area in typical mountain man hyperbole. "Pa'dners, I seed a pewtrified forest of pewtrified trees with their pewtrified limbs chockfull of pewtrified birds a-singin' of pewtrified songs."

Petrified trees choked the valley south of Twin Creek, so much so that early travelers had a difficult time winding their buggies between the sun-bleached stone trunks and branches. When Reverend David Long first settled in the area about 1871, he spent a great deal of time digging in the shale and collecting fossils. Atlanta (Long) Thompson wrote that "Professors from Colorado College came to see us once in a while and Father gave them any specimen of petrified wood, or choice of pieces of shale that they wanted. They hauled away many wagon loads of these specimens."

Hayden's 1873 survey of the area brought the geologist A.C. Peale to the Florissant

FLORISSANT FOSSIL BED'S FAMOUS BIG STUMP, a 500 year-old petrified sequoia tree. These three gentlemen had their photo made into a postcard around 1917--probably to impress a lady friend. *(Photo courtesy Marge & Don Christiansen)*

valley. Peale documented the scientific importance of the area when he later issued his report.

> About five miles from the mouth [of Beaver Creek, west of Florissant], around the settlement of Florissant, is an irregular basin filled with modern lake deposits. The entire basin is not more than five miles in diameter... About one mile south of Florissant, at the base of a small hill of sandstone, capped with conglomerate, are twenty or thirty stumps of silicified wood.

Paleontologist Samuel Hubbard Scudder followed Peale to the Florissant valley in 1877. He, too, was struck with the rich scientific material shallowly buried under the granite. He reported his findings in the 1882 "Bulletin of the United States Geological and Geographical Survey."

> The very shales of the lake itself in which the myriad plants and insects are entombed, are wholly composed of volcanic sand and ash, fifteen meters [over forty-five feet] or more thick they lie, in alternating layers of coarser and finer material...The insects preserved in the Florissant basin are wonderfully numerous, this single locality having yielded in a single summer more than double the number of specimens which the famous localities in Oeningen, in Bavaria, furnished Heer in thirty years. Having visited both places I can testify to the greater prolificness of the Florissant beds... and the quarries are fifty times as extensive and far more easily worked.
>
> ...Our examination of the deposits of this lacustrine basin was principally made in a small hill, from which perhaps the largest number of fossils have been taken, lying just south of the house of Mr. Adam Hill, and upon his ranch... Around its eastern base are the famous petrified trees, huge, upright trunks, standing as they grew, which are reported to have been five or six meters high [over eighteen feet] at the advent of the present residents of the region. Piecemeal they have been destroyed by vandal tourists, until now not one of them rises more than a meter [about three feet] above the surface of the ground, but their huge size is attested by the relics, the largest of which can be seen to have been four meters [about twelve feet] in diameter. The gigantic trees appear to be sequoias.

In addition to the interest expressed by Colorado College, various museums, universities, and prominent scientists continued to visit the site.

Pillage of the fossils and petrified wood was a cause for concern even as early as 1883.

A number of local citizens organized and incorporated the Colorado Museum Association. Keith Singer later recalled that one of the incorporators was none other than John D. Coplen. Of the $30,000 in capital stock that was raised, $8,000 was allocated for the purchase of Adam Hill's "Petrified Forest Ranch."

Coplen had made a fortune in copper mining in both Utah and Arizona. His interest in the Petrified Forest, however, was seen as more of a hobby than as a serious business venture. Nonetheless, the later actions of his Colorado Museum Association proved to be a source of alarm for the future of the fossil beds.

On August 16, 1883, the *Fairplay Flume* reported on the proposed plunder of the petrified stumps.

> ...a company has purchased for the sum of $7,000 the ranch upon which these great natural curiosities rest, and is about to remove one or more of them. As the fossilized stump which they are now operating on is altogether too large to admit of handling entire, being fifteen feet across the top and about the same depth to the bottom of the roots, it will be entirely cut up into sections of about two feet square, by means of steam saws, pure silica sand being placed in the cuts and serving the purpose of saw teeth. The stumps can be easily handled in this manner and will be shipped to some city museum and set up for admiration of thousands who might never see them in their native fastness. This is the only excuse that can be offered for marring the works of nature, and perhaps that excuse is ample.

Seven years later, in 1890, the Colorado Petrified Forest was still being operated as a tourist attraction. It was still owned by Coplen, as the 1884 article in Colorado Springs' *Daily*

Gazette indicated that the "good food and clean beds" at "Copeland's [sic]" were standard fare offered travelers. Admission to the Petrified Forest was 75 cents for adults and 35 cents for children, and "entitled each person to as many fossils as he has the patience to dig."

Exploitation of the stumps and fossils seemed a constant threat in the late 1800s. A reporter for the *Creede Candle* again sounded the alarm in a story on February 10th, 1893.

> The last remnant of the so-called petrified forest one and one-half miles south of Florissant is about to be taken to Chicago.
>
> The oldest settlers thereabouts remember that twenty years ago there were twenty of these petrified trunks standing erect besides numerous petrified logs lying over the ground. All have been removed by tourists and relic hunters until now one of the greatest and rarest natural curiosities of the world has been despoiled. The trunks and logs have been sawed up and broken to pieces and taken East, some intact to museums where they are regarded with great interest.
>
> The remaining trunk would have been removed long ago but for the great expense of the project. About twelve years ago parties from Denver undertook to remove the stump to the city as a museum curiosity. They worked a long time with horse-power and improved machinery, but finally had to abandon the undertaking. The Rocky Mountain Museum company has now undertaken to accomplish what the Denver people failed to do. Already the work has been begun by making excavations several feet about the roots so as to get as much of the roots as possible. This trunk is over forty feet in circumference and stands eight feet high. It will have to be removed in sections by sawing it lengthwise. The cost of its removal will be heavy and the company expects to reimburse themselves and make something by placing it on exhibition at Chicago.

There is no evidence, however, that the Big Stump was actually removed or exhibited at the Chicago Worlds Fair in 1893. The Big Stump prevailed, and ironically claimed the steel saw used to cut into its petrified wood, where it remains embedded to this day.

Unfortunately, some portions of these 500 year-old petrified trees were successfully removed and were shown in museums in London, Chicago, and Washington, D.C. Fortunately, fate intervened before the fossils and stumps were completely obliterated from the Florissant area.

Professors Farnsworth and Strieby of Colorado College in Colorado Springs arrived in Florissant in 1911 with a party from the British Museum. (If you will remember, Strieby was the Colorado College professor who analyzed the "gold" ore from Captain Hensley's potato patch in 1891.) Farnsworth was overawed by what he found. Farnsworth was quoted by the *Denver Post* as he effusively and eloquently reported on the fossil beds.

> ...This is the greatest fossil field in the world and I am afraid the people of Colorado do not realize what it means to the state and nation. We have come all the way from London to investigate these marvels, and if the fields were 5,000 miles away from here, Colorado Springs and Denver people would be paying their good money to visit them and wishing ardently that they were within the borders of this state. The fields are beyond justification the most remarkable in the way of fossil deposits in the world.

It wasn't until an article appeared in the *Denver Times* in 1915 that anyone suggested that the Federal government act to protect the "greatest fossil field in the world." The *Times* article focused on a report that the Federal Government had just established the Dinosaur National

Monument in Utah. Seizing upon the precedent which was established with this Monument, the

Times urged that the Florissant Fossil Beds also be made a national monument.

> ...Colorado possesses one of the most unique and best known
> fossil fields in the world, near Florissant. Fossils are discovered
> here in such numbers that a railroad runs special trains to this field
> during the tourist season. One is afforded the novel spectacle of
> hundreds of men, women and children diligently hunting the
> earth's surface and even digging in the ground, for the fossilized
> remains of antediluvian creatures...Setting aside these fields of
> fossil richness is in accord with the government's policy of
> protecting anything which is likely to prove of great public
> interest...Setting them aside prevents their location by individuals
> and their possible exploitation for gain.

Unfortunately, like the mythical Cassandra, the *Times* prediction of exploitation for

personal gain was later proven correct.

In 1920, David and his son, Ira Henderson, began a commercial venture that they called

a number of different names, among them Colorado Petrified Forest, New Petrified Forest, and

Henderson Petrified Forest. Parts of the Halthusen ranch home were moved to the west side

of the old Cripple Creek wagon road, and a pavilion and ticket office were constructed where

the park's visitor center is located today. A museum building was added in 1924, and was

operated until 1961. The Hendersons blasted out numerous stump formations, unearthing the

formation known as the "Trio" in their efforts. The principal exhibits of the Henderson Petrified

Forest were the petrified sequoia stumps.

Adjacent to this commercial venture, and slightly to the north, a second commercial operation was begun in 1922. John D. Coplen—who had ranched on the fossil beds since about 1884—moved the abandoned Colorado Midland Railroad station onto his ranch in July, 1922. At first, he used the old station as a ranch building. Later he converted it into a hotel, then sold it to Palmer John Singer on March 27, 1927, along with 160 acres of his ranch lands. Singer then acquired the adjoining property, known as the Chapman Place, just northeast of the Big Stump. Singer labeled his new ranch the Colorado Petrified Forest Ranch.

A bitter rivalry ensued with the neighboring, but unneighborly, Pike Petrified Forest when it was sold to H.D. Miller in 1950. His manager, John Baker, proved an eccentric and irascible operator. Agnes Singer recalled that "...Baker came over and tried to keep the tourists from coming into our place... he was spreading nails on the road and this [Singer tour guide] brought his gun and shot him." Baker soon recovered from his leg wound, but his rivalry had a new edge to it. He remained bitter, and availed himself of every opportunity to harass the Singers until the Pike Petrified Forest ceased operations in 1961.

Singer was a born promoter, however, and soon had his dude ranch filled with guests from all over the country. On Sundays, Singer conducted Professional Rodeo Cowboy Association (PRCA) rodeos with many of the day's big-name rodeo stars. Saturday night dances featured nationally famous entertainers. Guests who were averse to the clean mountain air and brilliant blue skies were given the option of filling their days, and emptying their pockets, in

COPLEN PETRIFIED FOREST RESORT in 1924. This picture was also made into a postcard which was then sent to Mr. & Mrs. William C. Allen at Twin Creek Ranch. Coplen moved the CMRR station house from Florissant to his petrified forest in 1922 and converted it into a hotel. *(Photo courtesy Marge & Don Christiansen)*

front of numerous slot machines in the hotel. Or, visitors could instead fill their pockets with fossils for the princely sum of 50 cents. In 1943, Singer again added more land to the Colorado Petrified Forest Ranch. This time it was Adeline Hornbek's old homestead, located along the northern boundary of the Colorado Petrified Forest Ranch.

Singer's ranch now encompassed what was reputed to be the world's largest petrified sequoia stump, measuring 74 feet around its circumference at its base, and standing a full 14 feet tall. Ranch guides escorted guests on a tour of the wonders of the ranch, including four other petrified stumps, a large petrified log, and Scudder's 1877-1879 fossil quarry site.

Singer continued to operate the ranch until his death in 1954. His widow, Agnes Ryan

Singer, and their son, Robert, then assumed control of the operation until 1973. Agnes had her troubles, however, as "Tourists began sneaking in and taking all they could carry." The Singers were concerned with preserving the fossil beds, fearing that "There'd soon be nothing left."

Finally, in 1920, the National Park Service began to take note of value of the fossil beds. Director Stephen Mather wrote that the fossil beds seemed worthy of national monument status, but that an examination needed to be made. However, it wasn't until twelve years later that such an examination occurred, and it resulted in an adverse report. Unfortunately, this negative valuation of the area as a national treasure continued until the middle of the century.

It continued into 1952, when Secretary of the Interior Chapman sent Yellowstone Superintendent, Edmund B. Rogers, to the fossil beds for an evaluation. Rogers culminated his visit by writing "Florissant Fossil Shale Beds, Colorado," in 1953. In spite of recognizing the "national significance of the Florissant lake beds to scientists," Rogers recommended against national monument status for the fossil beds.

A large part of this inertia was the perception that there was "no clear and present danger of loss of these interesting scientific features to the public." These early investigators felt that the Hendersons' and the Singers' commercial operations were doing an adequate job of protecting the fossils and petrified trees while still making them available to students and scientists and tourists.

It wasn't until 1962, however, that the National Park Service addressed the need to protect and preserve the fossil beds, finally acknowledging that they were endangered. A report by the National Park Service that year noted that "Even under the protection of the existing private developments, vandalism and promiscuous collecting of fossils continues..."

A report issued by Alberts and Knowles in 1962 (at the request of the Park Service Advisory Board) recommended that the area be preserved as a National Monument "as soon as possible." Their seminal report, "Florissant Fossil Beds National Monument—A Proposal" finally gave voice to the value of the area.

> The rare quality of the Florissant site lies not in dramatic exposures of big-boned creatures, but rather in the delicacy with which thousands of insects, tree foliage, and other forms of life— completely absent or extremely rare in most paleontological sites of this period—have been preserved. The fossils at Florissant are individually quite small, but in the aggregate are tremendous. Few fossil sites in the world have yielded some 60,000 specimens of over 1000 different species of life. In addition to this vast number of individual fossil specimens, is the remarkable way in which the fine-grained ash has preserved, in minute detail, delicate features of the innumerable specimens sealed within the layers of shale.

Dr. Estella Leopold, a United States Geological Survey paleontologist, wrote shortly after a visit in 1965: "If a single layer of paper shale in the Florissant beds could be uncovered simultaneously over its entire surface, we would have a detailed picture—a photograph in rock— of Florissant as it was some thirty-eight million years ago. As a volcanic tomb, Florissant is a kind of Dead Sea Scroll of evolution. There is simply nothing like it." In 1969, Dr. Leopold played a vital role in ensuring that Florissant's "Dead Sea Scrolls" would be preserved for posterity when she joined forces with the Defenders of Florissant.

Bureaucracies are lethargic, cumbersome animals, and the United States Congress is a prime example. Although a bill was introduced in Congress in 1963 to make the area a National Park, the bill was not voted on. A similar bill was introduced in 1965, but it also failed. In 1967, a third Florissant bill was introduced with an amendment to decrease the acreage from six to one thousand acres. This attempt at making the bill palatable by reducing the costs almost worked--the House passed the measure, but it again died in the Senate.

It wasn't until 1969 that a final, successful bill seeking to establish the Florissant Fossil Beds National Monument was introduced to Congress. In the meantime, however, a real estate development company had purchased 1,800 acres of fossil lands with plans for an A-frame housing development. Concerned conservationists from Florissant and other parts of Colorado banded together, organizing the Defenders of Florissant (DOF). As the developer's army of bulldozers rumbled toward the endangered fossil beds, the DOF sought an injunction. Led by Vim Crane Wright, a group of women drove up from Denver, prepared to lie down in the path of the bulldozers. Wright recalls dressing in a stylish outfit for the confrontation, certain that no bulldozer driver would run over a woman who was wearing pearls! Unfortunately, a federal judge ruled against the injunction, stating that it was a violation of the constitutional rights of the involved property owners.

Within hours of the federal ruling, however, the 10th Circuit Court of Appeals reinstated a temporary injunction against any further development of the fossil beds. This stalling for more time had been critical to the future of the fossil beds.

Three weeks later, Congress passed Public Law 91-60, creating the Florissant Fossil Beds National Monument. This final, successful bill was sponsored by Colorado Senators Gordon Allott and Peter Dominick, and the acreage was increased to the original six thousand. President Nixon signed the bill into law on August 20, 1969.

<u>Public Law 91-60</u>
<u>91st Congress, S. 912</u>
<u>August 20, 1969</u>

To provide for the establishment of the Florissant Fossil Beds National Monument in the state of Colorado.

Be it enacted by the Senate and House of Representatives of the United States of America in Congress assembled, that, in order to preserve and interpret for the benefit and enjoyment of present and future generations the excellently preserved insect and leaf fossils and related geologic sites and objects at the Florisssant lakebeds, the Secretary of the Interior may acquire by donation, purchase with donated or appropriated funds, or exchange such land and interests in land in Teller County, Colorado, as he may designate from the lands shown on the map entitled "Proposed Florissant Fossil Beds National Monument," numbered NM-FEB-7100, and dated March 1967, and more particularly described by metes and bounds in an attachment to the map, not exceeding, however, six thousand acres thereof, for the purpose of establishing the Florissant Fossil Beds National Monument.
SEC.2. The Secretary of the Interior shall administer the property acquired pursuant to section 1 of this Act as the Florissant Fossil Beds National Monument in accordance with the Act entitled "An Act to establish a National Park Service, and for other purposes," approved August 25, 1916 (39 Stat. 535; 16 U.S.C. 1 et seq.), as amended and supplemented.

SEC.3. There are authorized to be appropriated such sums, but not more than $3,727,000, as may be necessary for the acquisition of lands and interests in land for the Florissant Fossil Beds National Monument and for necessary development expenses in connection therewith.

Approved August 20, 1969.

BIBLIOGRAPHY

Books

Atherarn, Robert G., *The Coloradans*, Albuquerque, New Mexico: University of New Mexico Press, 1978.

Bird, Isabella L., *A Lady's Life in the Rocky Mountains*, Norman, Oklahoma: University of Oklahoma Press, 1988.

Cafkey, Morris, *Colorado Midland Railroad*, Denver, Colorado: World Press, 1956.

Carter, Harvey L., Editor, *The Pikes Peak Region*, Colorado Springs, Colorado: The Historical Society of the Pikes Peak Region, 1956.

Cassells, E. Steve, *The Archaeology of Colorado*, Boulder, Colorado: Johnson Books, 1990.

Conard, Howard Louis, *Uncle Dick Wootton*, Lincoln, Nebraska: University of Nebraska Press, 1980.

Conte, William R., *The Old Cripple Creek Stage Road*, Colorado Springs, Colorado: Little London Press, 1984.

Cragin, Francis, *Early Far West Notebooks,* Pioneer Museum, Colorado Springs.

Crofutt, George A., *Crofutt's Grip-Sack Guide of Colorado*, Omaha, Nebraska: The Overland Publishing Co., 1885.

Culpin, Mary S., *Historic Resource Study and Historic Furnishing Study -- Florissant Fossil Beds National Monument*, Denver, Colorado: U.S. Dept. of the Interior, 1979.

Cunningham, Chet, *Cripple Creek Bonanza*, Plano, Texas: Republic of Texas Press, 1996.

Dawson, Thomas R., F.J.V. Skiff, *The Ute War*, Boulder, Colorado: Johnson Publishing, 1980.

Dickinson, Anna E., *A Ragged Register (Of People Places and Opinions)*, New York, New York: Harper & Brothers, 1879.

259

Bibliography

Drannan, Capt. William F., *Thirty-One Years on the Plains and in the Mountains*, Chicago, Illinois: Rhodes & McClure Publishing, 1900.

Egan, Ferol, *Fremont - Explorer for a Restless Nation*, Reno, Nevada: University of Nevada Press, 1985.

Fetler, John, *The Pikes Peak People*, Caldwell, Idaho: The Caxton Printers, 1966.

Foster, Mike, *Strange Genius; The Life of Ferdinand Vandeveer Hayden*, Niwot, Colorado: Roberts Rinehart, 1994.

Grand County Historical Association, *Grand County Historical Association Journal*, Vol. VII, No. 1, June, 1987.

Hafen, Leroy R., Editor, *Mountain Men and Fur Traders of the Far West*, Lincoln, Nebraska: University of Nebraska Press, 1982.

Hafen, Leroy R. and Ann W., Editors, *Reports From Colorado, The Wildman Letters 1859-1865,* Glendale, California: The Arthur H. Clark Company, 1961.

Harbour, Midge, *The Tarryall Mountains and the Puma Hills*, Colorado Springs, Colorado: Century One Press, 1982.

Howbert, Irving, *Memories of a Lifetime in the Pike's Peak Region*, Glorieta, New Mexico: The Rio Grande Press, 1970.

Jefferson, J., R. Delaney and G. Thompson, *The Southern Utes*, Ignacio, Colorado: Southern Ute Tribe, 1972.

Kessler, Ronald E., *Anza'a 1779 Comanche Campaign*, Monte Vista, Colorado: Ronald E. Kesler, 1994.

Kimmett, Leo, *Florissant, Colorado*, Canon City, Colorado: Leo Kimmett, 1980, 1986.

Lecompte, Janet, *Pueblo, Hardscrabble, Greenhorn*, Norman, Oklahoma: University of Oklahoma Press, 1978.

Lee, Mabel Barbee, *Cripple Creek Days*, Garden City, New York: Doubleday & Company, 1958.

Madsen, David B., *Exploring the Fremont*, University of Utah: University Printing Services, 1989.

Marsh, Charles S., *People of the Shining Mountains*, Boulder, Colorado: Pruett Publishing Company, 1982.

McChristal, Jim, *A History of Florissant Fossil Beds National Monument*, unpublished manuscript in Florissant Fossil Beds National Monument possession, 1994.

McConnell, Virginia, *Bayou Salado*, Chicago, Illinois: Sage Books, 1966.

McConnell, Virginia, *The Upper Arkansas, A Mountain River Valley*, Boulder, Colorado: Pruett Publishing Company, 1990.

Noblett, Jeffrey B., *A Guide To The Geological History of the Pikes Peak Region*, Colorado Springs, Colorado: Colorado College, 1994

Olson, A.P., R.O. Roland, T.G. Bridge, *An Archaeological Assessment of Florissant Fossil Beds National Monument*, 1974.

Onis, Jose de, Editor, *The Hispanic Contribution to the State of Colorado*, Boulder, Colorado: Westview Press, 1976.

Pettit, Jan, *Utes, The Mountain People*, Boulder, Colorado: Johnson Books, 1990.

Rockwell, Wilson, *The Utes, A Forgotten People*, Denver, Colorado: Sage Books, 1956.

Roe, Frank Gilbert, *The Indian and the Horse*, Norman, Oklahoma: University of Oklahoma Press, 1974.

Ruxton, George Frederick, *Life In The Far West*, Norman, Oklahoma: University of Oklahoma Press, 1985.

Ruxton, George Frederick, *Adventures in Mexico and the Rocky Mountains, 1846-1847*, Glorieta, New Mexico: The Rio Grande Press, 1973.

Semple, Ellen Churchill, *Influences of Geographic Enviroment*, New York: Henry Hold and Company, 1911.

Bibliography

Smith, P. David, *Ouray--Chief of the Utes*, Ridgway, Colorado: Wayfinder Press, 1992.

Spell, Leslie Doyle & Hazel M., *Forgotten Men of Cripple Creek*, Denver: Big Mountain Press, 1959.

Sprague, Marshall, *Massacre*, Boston, Mass: Little Brown and Company, 1957.

Sprague, Marshall, *Money Mountain*, Lincoln, Nebraska: University of Nebraska Press, 1979.

Sprague, Marshall, *Colorado, A Bicentennial History*, New York, New York: W.W. Norton & Company, Inc., 1976.

Stewart, Alan J., Editor, *The Denver Westerners Brand Book - Vol. XXX & XXXI*, Boulder, Colorado: Johnson Publishing, 1977.

Thompson, Atlanta Georgia, *Daughter of a Pioneer*, Portland Oregon: Wayne Steward, 1982.

Utley, Robert M., *The Indian Frontier of the American West 1846-1890*, Albuquerque, New Mexico: University of New Mexico Press, 1984.

Whittemore, Loren R., *An Illustrated History of Ranching in the Pikes Peak Region*, Colorado Springs, Colorado: Gowdy Printcraft Press, 1990.

Wislizenus, Frederick A., *A Journey to the Rocky Mountains 1839*, Glorieta, New Mexico: The Rio Grande Press, Inc., 1969.

Winternitz, Barbara L., *The Mueller Ranch: A Unique Mountain Park*, Colorado: The Nature Conservancy, 1981.

Wood, Frances and Dodrothy, *"I Hauled These Mountains In Here!"*, Caldwell, Idaho: The Caxton Printers, Ltd., 1977.

Newspapers

Centennial (Georgetown, CO.)	1876
Colorado Springs Gazette	1884-1923
Creede Candle	1893
Denver Times	1900
Fairplay Flume	1883
Gazette Telegraph	1923-1937
New York Times	1874
Rocky Mountain Herald	1860
Rocky Mountain News	1875-1878
The Cascade Courier	1927
The Independent	1927 (?)

Bibliography

264

ACKNOWLEDGEMENTS

Writing this book has been a wonderful journey, and I am a bit sad now that it is ended. I could never have made this journey, however, without my best friend and companion, Harold, my husband. Of course, the writing would have been futile if I had not been able to coax the words from the computer, into the laser printer, and onto paper. Thank goodness my computer had a guardian angel, Chuck Mann, who made this all possible. I must also thank my children, who teach me something new every day--Melinda Gallop guided me through the intricacies of word processing and Jessica Hickman graciously allowed me the use of her computer.

My dear friend and advisor, Ed Eagle Man McGaa, helped to guide me through the labyrinth of publishing, and I am deeply indebted. My wonderful friend and amateur historian Kent Borgess gave invaluable advice. It then took the mind of a brilliant (but irreverent) college physics professor, Stephanie Di Cenzo, to ensure that there was logic and order in this book. And it required the analytical mind of a murder-mystery writer, Kari Wainwright, to keep me from murdering the English language too badly. All of these dear and dedicated friends have been vital to the successful completion of this book. I am also indebted to all of my friends in Western Writers of America, especially Chet Cunningham, for their encouragement and support.

Acknowledgements

Florissant artist Richard Thomas captures the spirit of the American West better than any other artist that I know, and Buck Venman integrated that art into one of the most attractive book covers possible. I am deeply indebted to them both for their impressive talent, and for lending it to this book.

Finally, this entire project was only possible through the generosity and kindness of the families of Pikes Peak backcountry pioneers. It has been an honor and a privilege to work with Judge Castello's grandson, Leo Kimmett and his wife Julia. I am also indebted to the great grandchildren of Count Louis Otto De Pourtales, Laura De Pourtales Clark and Chuck Walts. Also great-great grandson, Dan Pyzel. Virginia Pearce, Atlanta (Long) Thompson's grand daughter, and her husband, Douglas, have been extremely generous in sharing Atlanta's scrapbooks and photographs. Dr. Charles Snare's grand children have been exceedingly gracious and helpful, especially Rose White who copied numerous old family photos and her grandmother, Julia's, diary. Max Snare shared family history and genealogy, and helped me through the maze of Snare family land holdings until it became comprehensible, as did Al Snare.

I really began this journey in researching Twin Creek Ranch. Thank goodness that two strangers, Marge and Don Christiansen, stopped at the ranch one day, and shared the Allen family history. They generously and patiently loaned me invaluable photos of old Florissant, the Fossil Beds, the Allens, and Twin Creek Ranch.

I would also like to thank Sandy Sanborn, Helen Cahill, Mel McFarland, Midge Harbour, and Don Nichols for being so generous with their time and photos. Hugo and

Elizabeth Lackman of the Ute Pass Historical Society were wonderful for taking the time and effort to help me locate the many vintage photos of Pikes Peak backcountry. Maggie Johnston, Herb Myers, and Superintendent Jean Rodeck of the Florissant Fossil Beds National Monument provided invaluable corrections and comments. Doris Kneuer and volunteer, Wally Stark, were extremely helpful in research. Jim McChristal's comments and research documents were vital in providing accurate information on the history of the Fossil Beds.

Staff at Teller County Clerk and Recorder, Assessor, and County Treasurer's offices were invaluable in providing assistance for researching original records of the area. The staffs at Colorado Springs Pioneers Museum, Colorado College, Colorado State Historical Society, and Denver Public Library were efficient, pleasant, patient and helpful. I would also like to especially thank Alan T. Knight at Penrose Library for his very competent efforts.

Acknowledgments usually seem to be tedious things to read. However, nothing worthwhile is ever accomplished by one person. It is only because of the generosity of all of the people listed that this book has come to life. Thank you all so very much. Ten percent of the profits from *Pikes Peak Backcountry* have been designated for the Florissant Heritage Foundation for their excellent work in preserving the history and memories of the area.

INDEX

Hamilton, 19,99,103,122,160
Hamilton Road, 150,160
Handbury, J.E., 179,209
Handbury & Lentz General Store, 179-
    180,223
Haner, Henry, 133
Hardy, Amos, 242
Harker, Adeline, see Adeline Hornbek
Harker, Annie, 132
Harker, Frank, 132
Harker, George, 133,135,137,209
Harker, Simon A., 132-134
Harris, Claude, 204-205
Harris, Moses (Black), 11
Hartsell, Samuel, 120
Hawkins, Anne, 182-183
Hay Creek, see East Oil Creek
Hayden Divide, also see Divide,
    26,108,125,150,158,170,
    200,224,238
Hayden, Dr. F.V., 108,123-126,132,
    200,245
Hayden, Georgia, 188
Head, Lafayette, 100,102
Heer, 247
Heizer, D.N., Mayor of Colorado Springs,
    193
Hello Hotel, 201
Helper engines, 170
Henderson, David, 251
Henderson, Ira, 251
Henderson Petrified Forest, 251,254
Hensley, Captain John H., 210-214,
    219,227
He Who Picks Up Stones Running, 124
Hickman, Jack, 189-191
Highway 24, 30-31
Hill, Adam, 135,247-248
Hobo Mine, 210

Homestead Act, 3,99,126,132,236
Hoosier Pass, 146
Hornbek, Adeline, 132-138,151,
    155,160,235
Hornbek, Elliot D., 134
Hornbek, Elliot, 134,225
Hornbek Homestead, 109,253
Horrigan, John, 27,152
Horse, 7,33,39-45,50,51,56-57,65,72,74
Horse shoes, 45
Horsethief Gulch, 159
Houghton, Haddon, 227
Houghton, John, 227
Houghton, Mary McKinney, 147,227,230
Houghton, Richard "Uncle Dick," 147,
    226,227,229-231
Houghton, Tom, 227
Howard, George, 195-196
Howarth, Fred, 185
Howbert, Irving, 16,19,29,42,67
Hughes, Johnny, 88
Hugoton, Kansas, 179
Hundley, John, 24,223
Hundley Stagecoach, 24,215,223-224
Hunter's paradise, 92
Huntley, Paul L., 43-44
Hunt Treaty, 50,55,83,96,103,114
Husted, John Delano, 237

Ice Age, 7
Ice business, 202-203
Iliff, John Wesley, 120
Independence Mine, 216-217,240
Indian, 9,11-13,15-18,41,43,69,72,76-
    81,84,86-87,91
Indian Agents, 79,81,100,132-134
Indian Bureau, 99-100
Indian Fighter, 80